How to Calm the Fuck Down

DR. JASON COLE

DEDICATION

This book is dedicated to all those people who lose their cool. To everyone who freaks out over every little issue. To all the road-ragers and the people who just don't want to listen to anyone else during those heated moments. To anyone who generally makes bad decisions because they don't think things through. For someone who gets mad easily. For those who get an idea in their head and run with it, even when it's a bad idea! To those whose minds run rampant all day long with obsessive thoughts. To anyone who wants a little more clarity and mental focus. To people who want to be more productive. For anyone seeking an increase in happiness...

... this book is for you!

May you find peace and tranquility with an ease of mind in this life.

Dr. Jason Cole

CONTENTS

THANK YOU

I would like to thank the Universe for allowing what cosmic troubles it has had to go through in order to get us to this point in life that we are at today. I am grateful for the trials and tribulations of my early life growing up for it has made me who I am today, a stronger person. I would like to thank everyone involved with making this book become a reality and something tangible and real that you can hold in your hand, which seems to be quickly becoming a relic of the past. Thank you to my family and friends and especially thank you to all the haters who said this was a dumb idea!

INTRODUCTION

"This book is best read with a light southern accent, think Matthew McConaughey"

Look guys, I'm not gonna sit here and pretend to be one of you, because I'm not. I'm not gonna put on some jeans and boots with a plaid shirt and act like I'm your pal or your buddy. Because I'm not. I don't even know you and this is a book you're reading so I can't even see you from here!

What I am going to do is explain how meditation can help you out on job sites and make your lives a little more enjoyable while at work, and well, shit, maybe at home too!

I've done enough general labor in my life, shit jobs that nobody want's to do. I've dug ditches, I've cut down trees, I've built houses and barns, studding and drywall and even some plumbing; the shittiest job of them all and the whole time I've managed to keep a smile on my face.

You see, my dad wanted us kids to know what hard work was all about, what he called "A real-mans work" so that later on when we got off into life we wouldn't do any of that kinda work; backbreaking hard labor, toiling in the fields or working on vehicles.

Dad wanted us to go to university and get good high paying jobs that didn't take a toll on our bodies and health and that's why he was so hard on us out on the farm. Yeah, that and the free labor, am I right?

But what know what? Everything doesn't always go according to ol' dads plan in life and my brother and I ended up working a lot of these shit jobs over time. The reason that I say I am not one of you is because I hated every minute of those jobs. I hated the bosses, the people around me, the foul cuss words, the male chauvinism, the dinner bell whistle telling me when I can and cannot eat and especially the long twelve to sixteen hour days and putting in over sixty hours of work each week. And that's why I left that field of of work and have never returned. And so because I left I feel like I am not one of you, because you have all stayed. You have all put in the time, day after day, week after week and month after month and stuck with it to become good at what you do and I commend you on that. I never lasted more than 3 months doin these kinds of jobs.

Sure the money was good but where is that money today? It's gone! I spent it on surviving and keeping a roof over my head, a phone in my pocket and weed in my wooden pipe. So I'm not coming from a place where I feel like I'm above any of your or better than anyone, shit, I'm probably far worse off than any of you because I don't put in all that effort anymore. My bank account is empty and while I have food in my belly today there might not be any tomorrow but that is the risk I have embarked upon by becoming self employed. I no longer have the security of what you have and I often struggle some months just to pay a measly $500 in rent.

But I am happy. That's the difference folks. I am happy as a cat in a yarn factory on tuna-Tuesdays. And it's not like my life is all that more simple today. I still need to give physical exertion, I still need to deal with some assholes every day and I still need to bite my tongue to not say something that will come back at me later on. The difference is, that I now have the tools needed to run through this gauntlet, to be a warrior of the mind!

The first thing I wanna do is explain what this book is not about. It's not about telling you what to do. There are no guided meditations to follow with rivers and birds and weird hippie music playing in the background makin you fall asleep. It's probably the end of the day and you just worked your ass off and you're tired and you don't wanna fuck around with that shit. I know what it's like. You just wanna sit in front of the TV and get your Netflix on, right? Well hey man, nothing needs to change, you can still do all of that. This whole thing takes only ten minutes of your time in the morning and then maybe at night if you're up for it.

Have you ever gone to do somethin, maybe goin huntin or muddin with the boys or maybe just a family vacation and you needed to set that alarm a bit earlier than you'd like to get up, but ya did it anyways? Even though you knew you had a full day and it was going to be exhausting to the core but you still managed to get up and get goin? Well that's kinda what this is like, just an extra ten minutes and heck, you don't even gotta get outta bed to do this!

There are not going to be any practice sessions and there's absolutely no strict rules to any of this, you can take it or leave it, bit by bit. You find what works for you and you just run with it, or I guess you'll be sittin with it!

Learnin about meditation is a lot like buildin somethin, like a house. You see you gotta lay out the foundation first and then build upon that. There are certain tools to help you build the house and then once the house is built you don't need those tools anymore, you simply live in the house. But hey I know it's a good idea to keep a few tools handy in case something breaks down later on and we'll get to that too.

Our minds are here for one reason and one reason only, to solve problems. The mind is always seeking, always lookin for a new problem, somethin to fix! That's the nature of the mind. It's like "Where's the next issue: Where's the food? Where's the shelter? Who are my friends? What time is it? Am I late or not? Will there be a smoke break?" That is the mind. It's a little hammer always lookin for nails to bop on the head. And the thing about a hammer is, that it's a hammer man, everything starts to look like a nail after a while. The hammer doesn't wanna just lay back in the box it wants to fuckin hammer some shit!

The thing about the mind is, it's also like a blow torch, that burning fire! And you can't really put out the fire with another blow torch, and the same is said for trying to make the mind shut up by using your mind.

Problems, stress, worries and anxieties, that's all the mind is looking for and when they've all been tackled it just keeps looking and the small things in life start to turn into issues, into nails to bop! It's like you have everything in check, everything is perfect, your home life is amazing, your kids are perfect, your wife or husband is amazing and what he fuck is that little spot on the floor over there? Shit, I'd better find a way to remove that damn spot! And the next thing you know you've got half the kitchen floor dug up.

There's always somethin and there's always gonna be somethin so we're not gonna try and shut off the mind because that's pointless, shit you'd be dead if that happened! What we can do is learn to ignore it, learn to let it go, learn to love that damn spot on the floor if that's what it takes!

We need to step right out of that framework of attacking the mind and putting it down, because yes, it is needed for those real life problems too! You do need a place to sleep, you do need that food and those friends and that sex, that's all good shit for the mind to deal with.

A COUPLE STORIES

I'm gonna tell y'all a little story about cookin a pot of rice while visiting my mother. And man, she's like sixty somethin years old, my poor ol' momma didn't need any of this drama in her kitchen! But hey, it is what it is.

So like I said I'm cookin a pot of rice, and I suck at cookin rice, nine times outta ten it's gonna fuck up. But this one time I figured I had it. I put a timer on the stove and then I sat down across the room with my headphones on listening to Youtube videos. After what felt like like only a couple minutes went by I looked over at the stove and the timer was already flashing with 00:00 zero's and it was beeping like crazy! I didn't hear the shit beeping because of the headphones.

I went into some kinda instant rage as I flew across the room. In those few moments of busting my ass over towards the stove I thought about these things right here: I thought, why the fuck didn't my mom say anything to me about the beeping noise? I mean shit, she's just in the other room watchin some TV, like c'mon mom, help me out a little! I also thought about the stove itself cause it had one of those annoying glass-top systems that heat up all funny on ya, I was cursin and blaming everything under the sun, surely none of this was my fault!

But it was indeed my fault, I had put on those damn headphones and I didn't hear the beeping alarm from the stove. The thing is, when people get mad and it's their own fault they tend to get really mad! It's like if you knock this glass of water off my desk sure I'll be annoyed but I'll just say something polite like "Oh don't worry about, it's just water, I'll go get a towel". But if I were to knock that same glass over it's a whole other story,

5

then it's all "Jay you fuckin moron how can you be so fuckin clumsy and stupid and not being present and mindful and what the fuck is wrong with you?

Now all of these thoughts were happenin in the split seconds it took me to leap from my chair over to the stove and there it was, you guessed it, I burned the damn rice! And I yelled out loud "AHHH FOR FUCK SAKES!" But that was it. I caught myself in that moment. I saw my reaction for what it was, me being overly angry at my own headphone wearing dumb-ass, and I stopped myself. Well now my mother's attention has been gotten and she's in the kitchen tellin me to dump the rice out and just make some more.

Luckily upon closer inspection it was only the bottom layer that had burned and the top fluffy stuff was still good. The thing is, if I had not caught myself in that moment of anger, that little freak out time, a shit tonne of other things would have gone wrong; the food in the oven burning, the other pots boiling over, my phone goin dead cause the video was still playin on a low battery. If I had held on to that anger, and boy let me tell ya, there was a time when I would have held on to that anger for days; that kinda anger it just snowballs and it don't do nobody any good.

And this is why I need meditation in my life.

When you change only one letter in the word meditation from a T to a C we have medication. The two are very closely related. And what happens when people stop takin their meds? Yeah! They freak out man!

Okay I got one more little example for you before we get started! I dunno if you've ever looked up at space at night and seen a meteor shower happening or not, but it's quite impressive man. There's all these little fireballs, burning chunks of rocks shootin through the sky and it all looks pretty neat. I look at them and then I go back inside my house and forget about it. That right there is like meditating, if those meteors were your thoughts. It's all good from down here where we're safe on the earth, but up there in space, up in the middle of it all, those are giant flaming masses of rock hurtling through space destroying everything around them and the gravity of those giant rocks pulls other smaller meteors into their field creating an entire meteor storm! And you know what? Most people out there, that's where their heads are at, up in that storm. Where do you wanna be? Down here on earth or up in the storm? I prefer it here on earth myself.

There are so many things in this world that can piss us off into a frenzy of meteor shower thoughts. The car payments due tomorrow. The boss got mad at me yesterday. My brother is getting married. It's tax season next month. That fuckin guy cut me off in traffic this morning and it pissed me off and made late for an appointment! Gahhh! My belly hurts for some reason!

Whenever we think about the future we are always one hundred percent of the time making a projection out of possibilities based on shit that has already happened to us in our lives so far. But we can't really know the outcomes, we can only guess or project. So we gotta look at all these things, these meteors, from that safe space down here on earth.

The mind thinks about two things, the future and the past.

When we think about the future it's all projections that lead to fear, which cause anxiety and stress for something that has not happened and may never happen.

When we think about the past people rarely sit and dwell on the good time they had last week. Instead our thoughts usually gravitate toward something negative and sorrowful allowing it to repeat over and over inside our little noggins. It doesn't help that misery loves company and in our societies we tend to more easily bond over negative events. But the key point is that we cannot change the past so there's really no point on dwelling on it and revisiting it over and over. All we can do is move ahead, be mindful of the mistakes we have made and try not to let them happen again later on, but also don't project them into the future as a definite thing that will happen for sure.

Very rarely do we think about the present moment until it's affecting us directly like with a physical pain; a belly ache or a rock in your shoe.

You've all heard that saying to "Stop and Smell the Roses" correct? What do you think that's all about? It's about the present moment. You aren't think about your asshole of a boss and how he's going to be mad at you for being late (because you were smelling roses) and you aren't worried about the mistakes you made yesterday putting up those walls. In that moment all there is, is a beautiful flower, and a wonderful smell and maybe there's a bee in that flower so be careful we kinda need those things around for a bit longer!

A little bit of meditation each day is like stopping to smell that flower for just a few moments. Hopefully you've set your alarm ten minutes early so that you aren't actually late for work making that asshole of a boss too angry!

But why? Why do we even care? Why does any of this matter? Why can't we just simply live a life where we get all pissed off and angry every day? Why can't we worry about our futures? Why can't we cuss out that traffic dick-weed cutting us off? What is wrong with having our minds going a mile per minute popping off at every thought that occurs?

There's a couple different answers to this, first of all there is something called "cortisol" in our bodies and high cortisol levels are bad for you, like really bad. Meditation lowers those levels drastically. Coritsol is involved in stress and heart disease. It is involved in heart problems like high blood pressure issues, insulin spikes, poor sugar management and weight gain that affects our breathing, which, circles back to affect our heart again and the list goes on.

I know you all may think that you're a big strong man or woman and that you ain't afraid of nothin, but we do live in this fear-based society whether you realize it or not. Every little distraction causes our cortisol levels to rise. This is all leading back to our natural way of life living off the land thousands of years ago. When we lived in the forest and at night you would hear a twig snap your heart would jump out of its natural rhythm. You would be faced with a decision; to either run or stay and fight with an animal or an invader at your campsite! That pulse of energy that you got was linked to the cortisol.

So the other answer to this question about why we can't just keep being angry assholes all the time, is that our thoughts create the reality around us. If you have shitty thoughts all you're gonna see is shit everywhere. It's like the girl who stepped in dog shit and walked around all day thinking the entire planet was made of dog shit! You can imagine how happy she was when she got home and found that the entire planet wasn't made of dog shit, there was just a little bit on her shoe.

I'm sure you've heart it said to you, or you've said it to your own kids "Oh it's just your imagination, you're imagining things!" Well yeah man, it is *just* our imaginations! Our thoughts have imagined and dreamed up all of the miraculous stuff that we have here on earth. From TV's and cell phones to cars and airplanes, to power drills and air-nailers; it was all just somebody's imagination at some point. Those thoughts become a reality. So when you're thinking shitty thoughts all the time, shitty things and shitty people start to appear all around you and at some point your shit-addicted mind starts to see shit where there isn't even any shit at all and at that point, you're becoming lost.

And still again our thoughts do create another reality around us in the form or recognition. This has been proven time and time again with the Volkswagen Beetle phenomenon; that if you drive a Beetle you start to see Beetles everywhere! They were always there, you just never noticed them until you were also driving in one. This same phenomena happened to me when I drove a Toyota Corolla. I had never heard of a Corolla before I owned one then those fuckers were everywhere man! The same can be said for having a shit-addicted mind, we start to see shit everywhere.

Our thoughts get replicated, repeated and then expand in the mind. If you're on a constant treadmill running down a certain pathway. The groove gets worn deeper and deeper until you can only see the walls of the groove on either side of you. And now you're dug deep down into that trench in that one way of thinking.

Now here's the cool part. If you have trained your brain for joy and happiness, all you see is joy and happiness. You see it in others and you tend to look beyond the negatives, beyond all the bullshit!

The mind gets hooked on a track and you my dear readers can control that hook! But right now this track has been built up over time through our childhood development growin up in this fucked up world. Sometimes it's built up by our own experiences and by the people around us and their influences. Our minds are the way they are because we've been repeating, repeating, repeating the same things our entire lives. We have been, programmed. This all really wears that ol' groove in the brain and you get settled in there. After enough time has passed that groove is all that you know and it's your only way of existing.

People everywhere today have this increasing amount of obsessive compulsive anxiety and that is just something that happens naturally to anyone living in a fear-based society. When we remove the fear underneath it all a lot of these issues tend to melt away leaving your core values exposed.

So, what are your core values? Identify that shit! Make a list and post it on your fridge or tattoo it on your damn forehead. It's important to know what you want in life. This is a key step in starting to unclutter the mind and allow you, the deepest truest you in there, to make the decisions. Otherwise you're allowing the media like TV, movies, music or the news to influence you. And if you're one of those weirdos that doesn't partake in media, well guess what? The rest of the world does, and so everyone else around you whether you know it or not is makin that influence on you, on the media's behalf.

Alright, now that the foundation has been set, let's start to get some walls up on this thing! See you in the next section.

THE BENEFITS

LOWER BLOOD PRESSURE

All those damn doctors over here on our side of the world believe that our lifespan is measured by how many heartbeats we have, how long the ol' ticker will last. This is only half-true.

When we look at Eastern medicine they also value heart-health and all that but it goes a level deeper into the breathing. The breathing is what controls the heart and then the heart controls everything else.

The breathing regulation that is done while you are meditating causes the heart rate to drop. Long slow breaths in and long slow breaths out tells the heart "Hey! Slow the fuck down buddy, it's all good, we got this!"

The Western world has been designed, some say on purpose, to secretly work against us for breathing so that we stay sick and unhealthy.

Simply the way we sit all day hunched over causes poor breathing. Shit guys, I'm kinda hunched over right now typing this at my desk. I need to take constant breathing breaks by sitting up straight and taking a minute or two to allow those long full breaths to happen before I sink back into a slouch again.

So our chairs, our couches or sofas, the seats in our cars, on the bus, at work, in schools, waiting rooms and everywhere else are all designed so that you slouch in there, this puts a little kink in your body and you're no longer getting the right amount of oxygen into your lungs.

Now here is where this book starts to help you, but I'm not gonna just come out and say "Do this and do that" so you're gonna hafta pick and choose whatever little gems are dropped for yourself. You can pick up those little gifts or leave em' there on the ground, that's all up to you!

Smoking is a major concern, smoking of anything. Cigarettes and weed are both causing you to have poor circulation. I'm not knockin weed though man, I love some weed now and then but it's not an all-day every-day kinda thing for me anymore.

As it gets legalized in more and more places we are starting to see dispensaries popping up all over the place and we already know cigarettes are in every corner store out there. It's all part of this weird design to keep us sick (except the weed of course, quite therapeutic and medicinal in proper doses, but it does still affect our breathing).

You might think you live this healthy life and stay away from people who smoke and I do that too for the most part, but then the other day I was walking through a park and smoke was seeping out from the bushes! There were some kids in there puffin away on cigarettes and I ended up breathing in a big ol' lung full of that second hand smoke. So you can't really say that you're living a perfectly healthy life when there are so many outside factors you cannot control.

Vapes are in abundance these days drastically reducing the amount of oxygen going into people's bloodstream. I mean sure it's a healthier choice from all the chemicals in cigarettes but it's not helping your breathing out any.

And then there's things like pollution. You might not even realize you're being affected but when is the last time you sat in a traffic jam breathing all those fumes? I recently started riding a bike and nowadays bikes are regulated to ride on the side of the road next to all the cars. I noticed right away that my lungs were getting all fucked and I couldn't breathe from all the vehicle fumes. They say that riding a bike is supposed to be better for your health but then just look at the seat on a bike and the position of the handlebars and everyone's all hunched over again, breathing poorly and breathing in car exhaust.

So while we cannot stop all the kids from smoking in bushes, by not smoking ourselves and by being mindful of how we sit in these chairs we can learn to keep a straight and flat back which overtime will strengthen the back muscles. After a while you will notice that you no longer rely on the back of the chair to prop you up anymore but instead that you will tend to lean just a tad forward and hold yourself up, all the while getting full breaths, big lungfuls of air on a regulated pace that in turn are keeping your heart lowered.

LOWER HEART RATE

If your heart is always racing THUMP! THUMP! THUMP! THUMP!then it knows no other way of existing.

Now back when I was a dumb kid I bought a second hand car owned by an old lady. She never put it to the test out on the road so she never gave it the full Shazam! If you know what I mean? So when I got it out on the road for the first time by myself, a young teen, of course I tore the crap outta those pistons! Deep down inside the depths of the motor I knew little about those pistons had never been worked to know their full expansion and so over the years that they were in action they slowly wore a groove inside which eventually only allowed them to go so far. When that day came that I had taken it out for a good rocket launch the pressure tore apart all sorts of gadgets and gizmos inside as the pistons tried to shoot beyond the groove that had been built up over the years.

This is probably a bad example cause I don't want you over-stressing your heart so that you know what's under the hood, but what we can do is show it how slow it can go and show it that this is a possibility within its existence! Because the heart, that is caught in the groove cycle of beating fast all the time is a muscle and it knows no other way of existing.

By breathing those long slow breaths I keep talkin about for anywhere from ten to twenty minutes, the heart rate drops. If this lowered heart rate is only happening for the ten to twenty minutes or so that you are meditating in the morning then that is surely better than it not happening at all, wouldn't you say?

This process allows your heart to breathe so to speak, to know that there is another way of existing, while you are awake. It allows your ol' blood pumper to understand, through muscle and tissue memory, that there is another way and that life does not have to be all "THUMP!-THUMP!-THUMP!" and that it can also be a quieter "Thump... thump-thump. Thump... thump-thump".

We need to train that heart every day! It takes everyday consistent training as none of this is an easy quick fix. One does not simply meditate for an hour and have their heart rate fixed for the rest of their life. This is called a "practice" for a reason; you do it all the time – you practice it, over and over. Think about the first jig-saw you ever used, how well did that turn out? First time you ever mixed any cement? Or how about the first time you tried to put up some drywall? All of those things got better the more you practiced them over and over and it's the same shit with meditation.

And hey you're always gonna be changing bits and pieces about your practice so it's always gonna be getting a little better and it's gonna grow and change over time. Eventually that lower heart rate just starts to happen on its own and in your daily everyday life even after meditation is over. The great thing is that it says cool during those stressful times too, in those times when your adrenaline spikes and your heart's gonna beat right outta your chest!

REDUCED STRESS LEVELS

Do you even know what happens to you when you're scared? So let's say you're at work one day and something from high up above comes crashing down on the floor making the loudest KLAK noise you've ever heard. What happens to you? And I'm gonna get a little wordy here but hang in there.

Your hypothalamus, that's a tiny spot at the base of your brain, it sets off an alarm system in your body. Nerves and hormonal signals send a message to your adrenal glands above the kidneys to release a surge of hormones with shit like adrenaline and cortisol.

The adrenaline increases your heart rate, elevates your blood pressure and boosts your energy supplies. Cortisol, which I already talked about a little bit, is the primary stress hormone. Cortisol increases sugars (also known as glucose) in the bloodstream, so you are getting an insulin spike (like eatin a bunch of candy!) and it enhances your brain's use of glucose and increases the availability of substances that repair tissues.

Uhhh? What? I know right. Let me explain.

Cortisol cuts down on functions that your body doesn't need in a fight-or-flight situation. For example it shuts down your immune system and stops your digestive system, it shuts down things having to do with controlling your mood, motivation and even fear itself.

So if you have higher cortisol levels and all you are doing is sitting angrily in traffic or even upset about something you read online or whatever bozo dumb-ass said to you on lunch break, your body starts shutting down for no real immediate threat reasons. When the body shuts down for these things it affects our physical health and well-being.

I'm gonna just talk about food here for a minute. I have embarked on a ketogenic diet I'm sure some of you have already heard about it. It lets you keep eating all the meat you want, and all the salt and all the fat you want, the only thing you gotta give up, is sugar. All of it. You can't even eat something with any carbohydrates in them because that all turns into sugar! This diet keeps you fit as a whistle, muscles toned, weight down to nothing and feeling great! It's called becoming fat-adapted. So the body learns to burn fats instead of sugars for energy.

Once you've become fat adapted it's interesting that the brain no longer longs for sugars to provide the insulin spikes anymore when events start to unfold against your desire. When those fight-or-flight moments arise and you just want to explode into a fit of rage with your heart beating out of your chest, in those key moments your brain starts to say "Hey! Gimme the fats!" and so this allows the body to get into a new way of thinking. It lowers the amount of adrenaline, cortisol and insulin that is being produced in those fight-or-flight (stressful) moments by allowing you to get the energy you need without the damaging effects that come along with sugar energy. And, just a little side note here, fats contain three times more energy than what you get from sugars so you end up consuming less and having more energy.

When we're stressed the fuck out man, our bodies release these damaging enzymes into our muscle tissues in a sort of a high-impact high-acidic blast to jolt your body into running away from the perceived threat.

And again it goes back to that fight-or-flight response from living off the land. Like in the forest when you hear that twig snap at night and your body goes stiff and you are fully alert and ready to run away, or stay and fight an animal!

Our bodies cannot thrive in an acidic state, which incidentally is the perfect environment for cancers to grow.

So, picture this: It's late in the evening and you're sitting in your favorite armchair and you're half asleep, you're in that space between sleeping and waking. That space is highly suggestive, this is that space that hypnotists use. You're sitting there watching the evening news and it's bombarding your psyche with things to make you nervous, to scare you!

"Oh there is all this violence in the world!"
"Other countries want to attack us!"
"There are animals that will KILL YOU if you ever go off into the forest to try and get rid of your stress levels, don't go into the woods!"

So how does meditation reduce stress?

It changes the way you look at things, over time.

When we are meditating we see our thoughts go by and we let them just float away – and there will be more on this later! With a regular meditation practice this naturally starts to happen in our minds in our daily lives without us even trying.

So because it is easy to use as an example: You are sitting there in traffic (again!) and someone cuts you off (again!) and your anger starts to swell up (again!) only this time after having meditated you will see it coming. The anger is welling up "Ohhh no you didn't! Argh!" And there it is. Look at it. Recognize it. Maybe even label it "Oh, that's anger" and then watch it go by until... it's gone! No anger. It went right by and we did not get attached to it, we did not bring it into our realm, it just floated right by us and we are back waiting in traffic (again!).

INCREASED HAPPINESS

Who the fuck doesn't want to be happier? Am I right? If you don't want to be happy you can just close this book right now because it's gonna start happening as a simple byproduct once you start practicing this shit.

This kinda goes back to a previous section about lowering your stress levels. Lower stress and happiness are sorta partnered together, one happens after the other.

To put this as plain as punch a little meditation that reduces your stress will also lead to an increase in happiness. The ability to spot our thoughts and watch them as if they were not our own and see them float by allows us to see our positive thoughts as they happen, and we also watch them float by too. Now what are we not gonna do with those happy thoughts? I'm speaking about the previous section on attachment here, that's right, we are not gonna get too clingy with those happy thoughts either cause that just causes a fuck-tonne of problems down the road when you become burdened with trying to hang on to the happy times for too long.

An example about this sort of shit happening is maybe you're going on a vacation. Maybe it's not even a vacation maybe it's a hunting trip with your buddies and you just found out it's happening, and even better, you're invited, and even better, you ain't gotta pay for shit-all so it's all free! Well hot damn! That excitement is gonna build up inside you ain't it? Fuck yeah it is! But hey, this ain't happening until six months from now.

So you got that little excitement in your heart. Every day you're out there grinding it at work. You're strugglin away and everything sucks but at the back of your mind you know that in a few more months you'll be on that trip. And right there in that moment, your brain starts to fantasize about the future. You start thinking about the four-wheeler and the mud spraying up in your face. You're thinkin about reaching back to grab a cold frosty beer and cheersing it with your pals. You're thinkin about the smell of the gun goin off and the exhilarating adrenaline that follows when you land a deer or whatever the fuck you're out huntin for crashes to the ground. You're thinkin about all these happy times, and man, they haven't even happened yet! So like, wow, imagine when they do happen, right? It's going to be intense!

Six months of dredging work seems to just float by as you continue to think about all these amazing things that are about to happen. You and your buddies finally embark on that road trip. Halfway there your buddies SUV breaks down and has to be left behind while all the supplies are loaded into the other jeeps and trucks, so now it's a bit of a tight squeeze. The new guys you're driving with don't like smokin weed in the vehicle like you were before in the SUV so that's out of the game until you stop someplace, but hey, just a minor setback. You all arrive at the destination, a small cabin y'all have rented from a fella online. The cabin is out in the forest, deep in the forest. You met a man at his house on the way in and he drove everyone to the cabin. You get inside the cabin and there's two less beds than what they said in the advertisement so two of y'all need to sleep in the truck. There's no running water so you need to use the well-pump or the river but the river has pretty much dried up because it's out of season. There's no electricity in the cabin and no fridge to store all the beer y'all had brought with you and to make it all the more interesting the shitter is outside in its own little outhouse box. At this point you're thinking about going home and saying "Fuck this shit" because it's not what you signed up for at all six months ago.

You're feeling mighty down and upset, the other boys are upset and feeling the same too and none of this experience is going right, or going the way you had thought it would. The way you had projected.

You see, thoughts about the future are just that, thoughts. The mind likes to project and invent some shit that hasn't happened yet. It invents shit either the way you want or expect it go to down, or it invents shit in the most negative way with all of the disasters that "could" happen being just around the corner, and it projects shit based on your own life experiences and how things have happened to you in the past.

So what the hell has happened to your vacation you have been thinking about for the last few months? This is what happened: Over the last six months from the minute you found out about the trip you started being overly excited about it and you started to borrow from the excitement that should have been happening during the trip. In fact you tapped into that excitement every day for the full six months as a way to mask your shitty life at work. You been talkin about it every day, you been daydreaming about it every minute and you literally bled it dry! It's like you time traveled into the future and stole the excitement to bring it back with you to your shitty days, to sort of make those days a little more enjoyable.

At this point, you're out there in the woods now, and life still sucks. So ask yourself, was all that daydreaming worth it? Was it worth stealing the excitement from the future? And because this is how you do things, this is how your brain works, you steal from the future and you start doing it again out there at the cabin. And you start projecting into the future saying "Oh I can't wait to get back home again in my own comfy bed!" and so the cycle starts over again. You might not be thinking about your comfy bed but you might be thinking about telling the stories about this trip in an excited way, all the trials and tribulations you went through during this vacation, maybe to get a little pity from others or maybe to keep a machismo ere to your adventure. And you might even retell the stories in a way to make the trip seem like it was actually a lot of fun for everyone involved. So, what do we do to prevent all of this from happening? We walk the middle line, we take the path that plateaus.

So let's rewind to six months ago and you're being invited to the trip. Rather than get all hot and horny about it you just kinda put it away on the shelf and go about dealing with your shitty everyday life as best as you can.

Don't get too excited, and don't get too down about things. This is the middle path.

Now let's fast forward to the trip. The SUV breaks down but it's no big deal. This is just a small challenge squeezing everyone together and you start to see that it's actually better that y'all ain't smokin weed while driving because there was a roadblock and y'all woulda been in some deep doo-doo.

The cabin doesn't seem like such an obstacle, y'all quickly figured out that you wouldn't really be doing that much sleeping anyways and could sleep in shifts or take turns using the truck and beds. Everyone agrees it's not about the luxuries of life, it's all about getting back to your roots and roughin it out in the forest the way the hunters did back in the day. You weren't really gonna use water for anything cause all you brought was disposable cutlery and plates with some junk food with you and you figured out that you could put your beer down in the little bit of river water that would keep them cool enough to drink. Dealing with the bullshit as it arises is the way to walk the middle-path. Escaping through projections is not the way and only leads to more problems later on.

One of the main points is that we are seeing our thoughts for the first time rather than allowing them to control us simply because they are there. It don't matter if they are positive or negative.

It is like that boss that walks into the room and everyone's anxiety goes through the roof as he starts barking orders and expects everyone to jump! We can watch that boss walk in, we can hear his words, see his physical frustration by the vein poppin outta his forehead and then we can debate whether or not we should jump, and how high to jump. There is always a middle ground to exist within.

When we are caught-up in jumping for the boss or even jumping for our own thoughts, and it goes both ways from excitement to drama, we fail to see the middle ground. When we jump too high we also fall harder coming down.

So you're having a good day? Or maybe you're having a bad day? The excitement is fleeting and it don't last. The drama is fleeting too so it won't last either. Both of these things come and go all the time and it's happening all around us every day only you aren't realizing it is happening because you're being focused on your current good or bad day. Or maybe today you are on that middle ground and you're wondering why it's such a dull and boring afternoon? The thing is, it's really not. All the excitement and drama is all still there only you aren't in tune with it so you're not seeing it, but it's all still there.

It's like some days the hammers and pipe-wrenches are flying through the air and you don't have a care in the world as nothing seems to phase you. Meditation can get you into that mind-frame and keep you there, every day!

I just wanna warn y'all that if your boss only has you around to jump for him and you stop jumpin, you're probably gonna get fired! On a positive note this opens up your life to new possibilities where you can explore a more positive employment option better in tune with the new-you, with the the new middle-ground version you are becoming.

And this is the scary part folks, people often want a change but they don't want anything to change. It's like they want things better at work when it's just the pure nature of that shitty job that it will never get any better. Then the change comes and it's in the form of a job loss and you're forced to go do something else. This is the time where you get to make a choice.

This is your existential crossroads! You can either go back down the old path toward the same sort of bullshit you have been putting up with or you can find a new path to walk down. I know jobs are scarce in most parts, skills are tailored toward maybe one or two things and that can make us feel trapped like we have no other options, but these are just... you got it! Your own thoughts! Don't get attached to those thoughts.

And even just as important is that you don't get caught up in other people's thoughts about what you should do either. You may have realized your own self-actualization happening and yet your wife don't want you to quit your job so she's gonna say a lot of stuff that's gonna burrow deep into your psyche, maybe even deeper than your own thoughts were and so you cannot allow other people's opinions to hold you back.

Now, the other weird thing that might happen is this, you don't even think about quitting your job, but as the days go by and your inner changes start to happen that boss has noticed you aren't jumping as high anymore and he might fire your ass over it. Sometimes it just happens. The other possibility is that someone else who is already on the next level of vibrations, playin the next game over in another field is gonna see you over there grindin away in the dirt and they will approach you with an offer to come check out greener pastures!

Anyways, once you get the hang of some of this meditation stuff, you'll see the increased happiness start to happen in places that you never expected it to happen!

AN INCREASE OF FOCUS

So if you wanna be technical about it, this focus aspect is not one hundred percent from the meditation but it's a small part of it. Later in this book you'll see some of the various focusing techniques that will help ya out when you're doin the damn thang!

Meditation helps you stay with it. It helps you stay alert so that you'll see those hammers flying through the air! It helps you stay present in the now, in the moment, so when you're walkin across that scaffolding you're not thinking about what's for dinner when you should be keeping an eye on your footing. It helps you see things for what they really are. Maybe you're being asked to do something a little dangerous that maybe they shouldn't be asking you to do, you'll be able to spot that kinda shit right away! If you're better able to pay attention to the world around you, you'll have an easier time doing some of the more simple things like crossing a street or driving in traffic, or fuck man, even something more complicated like not getting eaten a bear in the woods.

Focus is also good for being able to take part in a proper conversation. Because man, and I'm tellin ya, whether you know this or not conversations have ebbs and flows, ups and downs, ins and outs to them. It's not just one guy barking orders all the time and one person listening. It's also not listening to respond.

So a conversation has this push-pull thing happening. I say something and you say something. I have the power and then you have the power. I take the power back then you take the power back. It's kinda like a game of catch ball in a field if ya 'catch' what I'm sayin?

So how the fuck does meditation help with all this shit? Well, by keeping a clear mind during these conversations we are able to really tune in to exactly what the other person is saying. Our ability to listen is increased as our mind is no longer flooded with thoughts about something to respond with. A fuck-tonne of people out there are only listening to respond. They don't really care what you are talkin about, they are just waitin for their chance to say somethin and so they don't really listen, they just kinda skim over it waiting for a key-word here and there.

For example, if I'm talkin about elbow pipe joints and you take a mental note about pipes so you can reply to that when it's your turn to speak, then shit man, that's just great! If your mind was too busy you might have only grabbed as the word elbow and started rehearsing a story about the time you bumped your elbow and your funny bone went all wonky, then you're not really doing any good for either person are you?

There are a wealth of focus techniques online for you to try out, some are like fun games, and some are very simple to do with just a pen and a paper. And we will go over a few of these later on in the lessons.

THE BENEFITS OF A RELAXED MIND

The brain is a muscle constantly being over worked, over flexed!

What would happen if I as a child fresh out of the womb started flexing my arm all day and every day? Like this... GRRRR! It is going to develop poorly. It is going to be all weird and deformed and how can I even go to the washroom? Or type? Or lift a hammer to throw at someone? It is a hindrance to have a constantly flexed muscle in this way.

Your brain is a flexed muscle all day right now and this world we live in will tell us that we need to keep a flexed brain for protection or the forest monsters will get us! The world says that we need to be in total control of everything all the time and we know this ain't even possible because a damn satellite could fall from the sky and crush us at any moment. So you really have no control at all, forget about it, and let that shit go!

The world says to never stop flexing that brain muscle! Think about this! Now think about that! Now play these mind games with people! Now act a certain way to be here in society! Now act a different way when you're with your buddies drinkin beer! Now act another way with this lady friend! It never ends!

But, we do not live in a jungle anymore and we are relatively safe. When we are in this old way of thinking our minds can get into that fight-or-flight response and the cortisol levels increase and that shit just ain't needed anymore! But hey, if you're down in a known dangerous place of the city you should have some wits to get on outta there if true danger arises, otherwise we do not have any predators after us out there.

LET IT GO

Meditation trains the mind to have moments of peace, moments of release, moments of not being flexed. After practicing for a while your mind will start to relax and be less tense about every stupid little situation that comes up.

I have written novels and thousands of songs. I had a chattery mind that would not shut the fuck up for days on end! I always believed I had to write everything down and that I had to do every whim, every passing thought, every little inkling of an idea had to be transcribed in some way either onto a cell phone or paper then later onto a computer. And for what? In the end I had thousands of notepads full of little blurbs of notes and ideas and sayings and song lyrics or short story-line ideas that never made it anywhere else other than those notepads that are now all in the trash.

Meditation trained me to let it go. I can now have a million killer ideas float through my head-space every day and not one of them needs to be written down like I used to. My mind just see's the thoughts, they float by and I wave at em "See ya later fuckers!" If they are truly important they will return when the time is right and at the right moment, not before and not after.

DON'T GET CAUGHT-UP

But caught up in what?

In anything really. When you get caught-up, attached or obsessive over something it begins to hold a power over you. It is important to learn to spot the things you are caught-up in and a little meditation will allow you to see these things quite clearly as they occur.

Like right now I'm caught up in this art project and I'm trying to get it all packaged up and sent out to the shops to be sold. And ya know what man? It's all I think about. It is taking up a lot of real-estate in the ol' thought streams lately.

I was caught up in the music industry for many years. I remember countless nights when friends would ask me to join them on some sort of fun adventure, probably camping in the woods, and I would snidely bark at them snapping "I'm working on my ALBUM!" like it was the most important and most profound thing to ever be written. As though it was some masterpiece of genius work that would be honored in a museum for all eternity. Eventually the album got a one star review on iTunes and was forgotten about. So you see, a lot of life experience points were missed because I was caught-up in something that I held dear to my heart that was really in the end only holding me back from growing further as a person and from experiencing life and enjoying my friendships. And the whole time the universe was right there trying to grab me and shake me out of it and get me out of the house to actually live and get something real to write about!

It is quite easy to get caught-up even in things that at the time seem like they are the most important things about our lives. A little mindfulness would have helped in my situation back then as I could have spotted these times when I was ignoring life to stay in the trap of music.

On the other hand, being a musician did bring me to some amazing places and I met some great people and even made some lifelong friends. However, looking back at it now I can clearly see just how much I had missed out on. For a long time after the music and local bar-star fame had ended I was a little disgruntled and a little cynical about the music industry.

I held it in my heart that the entire industry was fake and full of slithering snakes and social climbers who pretend to be your friend just to use you as a stepping stone for the next level, a level that never seems to ever arrive, for either of us. I have had to let all that go to appreciate and have gratitude for what it did give me, like the ability to get on a stage in front of thousands of people with the confidence to entertain and perform where previous to that I had a crippling stage fright.

Maybe music is not your trap, maybe you are into baking or sports-cars or maybe you like to collect things and are a hobbyist, building model trains, collecting Pokemon cards; all of these things have been designed on purpose to hold our attentions and keep us away from what is really important in life, and that is, truly living our lives to the fullest and utmost capacity and wonder in a state of love and compassion.

Hobbies are great to have, yes, as long as they don't start to creep in and control your entire life! Music for me started out as a hobby and slowly took hold over every move I made. There were times when I wouldn't eat because I needed that money to buy cd's to hand out at a show. Some people look at this as dedication yet when you are denying your own existence and suffering at a home level and not taking care of yourself it has become a sickness.

Look into your own lives and see where you are caught up and see what sickness levels of attachment you have to your own ideas, values, morals or even just the things you like to do, maybe it's video games or riding horses! I don't fuckin know, but I'm sure there's somethin in there if you dig deep enough! Once you have realized your unhealthy attachments you are able to draw some solid line and say no to overstepping the boundaries and bring into place a healthy balance of work, life, friends and hobbies.

And again, just to bring it all back to what this is about, a little ten minutes of mindful meditation every morning allows you to be clear and focused during the day to maybe spot some of these attachments.

TRIED AND TRUE TECHNIQUES

Alright folks, we are getting down to some real shit now. This is where the whole thing really begins. This is where I'm gonna teach y'all about some different ways that other folks have been meditating for thousands of years. The only reason I have chosen these techniques is because it's been working for a shit-load of people around the world. I said this before though, if you don't like it, don't fuckin do it! If you do like, keep doin it.

Sometimes you're only gonna like one thing from these different styles and you're only gonna take one thing from them and merge that into your own custom style. So stick with the little bit of reading until the end and then come back and try whatever looks the most interesting to you. By at least trying them you can find out which little piece is the right fit for you and your lifestyle.

And just and FYI, some of the technique names might sound like some hippie trash but hopefully you can overlook that bullshit if you've made it this far into the book already!

We are going to explore Shambhala Buddhist Meditation, Transcendental Meditation otherwise known as Mantra Meditation, Kundalini Meditation, The Moment Meditation and My Personal Meditation with notes on how it has grown since I started doing the Mantra Meditation. You'll read about the Loving Kindness Buddhist Meditation, Zen or Zazen Meditation and we will talk a little bit about Binaural Beats which are these sounds that pretty much just help you cheat and skip over the hard part!

SHAMBHALA BUDDHIST MEDITATION TECHNIQUE

This was taught by a man named Chogyam Trungpa who, despite all the negative things people try to say about him, a lot of good came out of him as well. Ya see, this man was a Guru of sorts, a teacher, and he was a drunk who loved women and food. He loved all kinds of shit that other teachers would shake their heads at, mostly because his teachings were all about walking the path of the warrior and being impeccable in every aspect of life.

All these so-called negative things ended up being part of his method of teaching. Chogyam brought this meditation style to the Western hemisphere. Trungpa opened up meditation centers all across North America many years ago, some of which still run today, with their flagship center being in Nova Scotia, Canada, where I am from.

In this meditation, the meditators are urged to sit on comfy cushions and bolsters, or in a chair with their feet on the ground. There is a little bit of ceremony involved as they have someone who is the Time Keeper and this person leads the meditation with some incense burning and some bells or gongs to signal the starts and ends of the sessions. Meditators minds will wander and they are always urged to return to the breath. Follow your breathing. In and out. In. and out. Just like the waves of an ocean rocking you gently into a trance-like state.

Most practitioners do this meditation with their eyes wide open always staring out at the ground at a forty five degree angle to about three feet in front of them. This is however not a requirement, the meditation centers do not have any strict guidelines; they ain't gonna kick you out if your eyes are closed!

Half-way through the session everyone gets up off of their ass and begins a walking meditation. Eyes are open for this walking. You do not look around the room or at other people you just keep your eyes focused on the floor directly in front of you at the heels of the person ahead of you as everyone walks around the room several times for roughly ten minutes. So you're still following your breathing. In and out. In and out. The idea is to involve more of your body mixed in with the meditation to train your body, your muscle memory that it is possible to be in a meditative state while you are up and doing things.

A lot of people think that meditation will only help you while you are meditating and this is not the case. As for your thoughts, with Shambhala

Buddhist Meditations, you really get deep into the introspective aspect of your thoughts. As soon as some shit comes up, you fuckin deal with it. You don't let it take you for a ride and you don't try to push it away. So you work through them, pass them along and allow them to fade. Once you realize that you have been thinking too much you simply return to the breath. This turns into a form of self-therapy.

Many people have broken out into tears during these meditations and some people need to get up and leave the room. Don't try to be a macho man, just get the fuck up and leave the room so you don't annoy everyone else in there. It's totally cool if you leave and besides nobody else is going to know why you are leaving, maybe you just need to go take a fat shit! And yes, these are generally practiced in a room full of other people around you.

My personal experience with these Shambhala Buddhist people was a little bit different than what most folks seemed to have had with them. At the time I was in a phase where I was strongly relying on Binaural Beats to ascend me to a higher level, to jump start my meditations by about twenty minutes in, and get right into a good head-space. The Shambhala people thought this was cheating and that I was not doing the work. I was not dealing with any of the things that arise and just jumping right into the whole scenario before I technically should have been allowed to.

TRANSCENDENTAL (OR MANTRA) MEDITATION

HEALTH BENEFITS OF TRANSCENDENTAL MEDITATION

There are an abundance of studies around the health benefits of Transcendental Meditation. In a nutshell, T.M. Has been found to:

Reduce metabolic syndrome, manage the effects of trauma, extended longevity, lower blood pressure in at-risk teens, reduce atherosclerosis, reduce thickening of coronary arteries, reduce myocardial ischemia, manage and prevent anxiety and helps manage cholesterol.

Whenever you hear about scientific studies on meditation with like all these brain scanner machines, these studies have all been funded by the T.M. organization.

I am going to take a quick second here to explain a study that was done by the T.M. org's hired scientists where an experiment was carried out one hundred times where two thousand meditators came together in one city for a week to meditate. What happened was the crime and violence rates dropped through the floor. The study also investigated a phenomena when there is a big mixed martial arts fight or a boxing match in a city, violent crimes increase by eighty percent in some areas during the week leading up to that event.

What the scientists also learned was that by placing two pianos across from each other in the same room and pressing on the C note on one piano, the same C note string on the other piano vibrates and this is also happening within us humans. So when one large group of people are all riled up and angry it promotes the same vibrations in others around them and so when you have peaceful group of people meditating it begins to affect the others around them as well.

Electroencephalography (EEG) is used to show brain activity under certain psychological states, such as alertness or drowsiness.

Positron Emission Tomography (PET) scans show brain processes by using the sugar glucose in the brain to illustrate where neurons are firing.

Okay, what?

Yeah, they hook people up to these things to have their brain scanned during meditation and after meditation. Then they hooked it up to people who never meditate and each time the results come back that the people who do meditate have a higher functioning brain.

So what in the fuck is T.M.? I honestly feel like T.M. is the meditation technique for the regular everyday Joe. The sad part is that none of the regular folks can afford to take the classes! You see, this is that shit you hear all the celebrities talking about. Russell Brand, Ellen, Hugh Jackman, Jerry Seinfeld, Jim Carrey and a slew of others who have gotten interested in it, or maybe they were hired as celebrity endorsements because of David Lynch, a prominent Hollywood actor and director who now runs the T.M. organization? Who really knows?

What we do know is where it all began. There was a man from India a long time ago named Maharishi Mahesh Yogi. This motherfucker went to California where he started teaching T.M. shit for a hefty fee! His story was that his teachers back in India told him to go to the West to do this. Later research showed that Maharishi never had any instruction to go teach this to the Western world and the higher-ups than him in India claim that his entire technique is bullshit. They say it's sort of like what they teach, but not really, that it's been twisted in a way to keep people coming back for more and paying another fee for an upgraded lesson.

The damnest thing about this story is that his technique actually works, for a short while anyways until you need that upgrade, but we'll get to more of that later.

So Maharishi started getting all this money piling up. He lawyered up and became a corporation; a business man. He started having lots of sex with his students and buying fancy cars and mansions. But nobody seemed to care because his technique worked and this is a capitalist country, that's what it's all about right? Buying shit, and having lots of sex! Enough about this guy though because after he got run out of town for eventually being found out to be a fraud another man named David Lynch took up the reigns over the T.M. Movement and started what you see now at www.TM.org. The organization charges upwards of $1000 to learn the technique today. But, we can't really get mad at them for making a dollar or two off of this shit because they put so much money back into the scientific studies that it helps all the other styles of meditation become more relevant, modern, mainstream and accessible to the public.

Okay, so again, what the fuck is T.M.?

This is quite simply, a mantra meditation and a mantra is something that you repeat over and over. The word mantra can be broken down into two parts, Ma means Mind, and Tra means Cleanse. Mind-Cleanse. A mantra can be just one word or a few words and sometimes it's got a little melody or a jingle to it. As I said a minute ago T.M. is run by a group that can be found at www.TM.org is you would like to reach out and learn the technique directly from them.

The T.M. Course lasts four days. Each day's class is one hour long and during the first day you meet with and talk to your instructor who gives you your special word, your mantra. Supposedly the mantra has been selected just for you by your teacher. I later found some documents from the organization outlining how the words are selected based on your gender and birth date. The words they use are Sanskrit words from the Vedas (ancient texts) used to name the many Hindu Gods. You are not meant to tell your mantra to anyone; it is yours and only yours, if you so choose. You are encouraged to never look up its meaning because if you know what it means that's all you'll be thinkin about during the meditation as you repeat that shit over and over.

For a beginner T.M. sessions are twenty minutes in the morning and twenty minutes at night while the advanced folks do an hour and a half in the morning and at night. Yep, that's three hours of their day spent meditating! Who the fuck are these lucky folks with so much time on their hands? Oh! Right! Celebrities!

The meditation starts before you do anything at all, no food, no drink, no cell phones, no talking to anyone. You just hop up outta bed and go sit down for the time needed. At night it's done right before you go to bed and once it's done, no talking, no cell phones etc., just go straight to sleep.

Okay, so you don't have a mantra given to you by a teacher, now what? Well, y'all can do what I did. I wrote down a bunch of syllables on pieces of paper and drew three from a hat. I came out with Ra, Ma and Sa, in that order. So that has been my T.M. mantra since I started. It has zero meaning and I don't care if anyone else knows about it or uses it.

So yeah, when you first start this shit repeating the mantra in your mind over and over, well, that's all you're gonna have and you're probably gonna pat yourself on the back for being so damn good at repeating a word! But that's not the end of it. Eventually you'll have your word playing on a loop and then some other shit's gonna start to come up and wholly fuck! You're right back at it again with all that pesky thinking noise about your job and car payments and kids needing new shoes!

So now what do you do? Well, don't panic, this is all part of the process. As soon as you catch yourself thinkin about the bullshit again, that's your chance man, this is when you go back to focusing on the word again, so it all kinda starts over again.

Don't get all upset and pissy with yourself if you're having some other thoughts happen because that's all natural and it's all part of it man! Just simply start over.

Now here's some weird shit, the mantra doesn't have to be perfect. It can and will take shape and other forms. Like my word for example started out very specifically as Raaaaaaa Maaaaaa Saaaaa. Later it got shorter to RaMaSa, and even still it would switch over to sound more like RAMmmmmmm-ASA! So just kinda let it go where it needs to go.

This is one of those things that is hard to describe with words and is understood after you have experienced it for yourself, but eventually the mantra and the thoughts both fade away as you "transcend" into the fully blissful state of relaxation, pure meditation.

But what is that? How do you describe that state so that you know when you're there? Well, you can't really. You can only tell when you are not there. And you are not there when you are consciously reciting the mantra, or when the overload of thoughts is happening. When neither of those are happening, you're not able to perceive the lack of it as time just sort of skips by, but it is those moments that are key. You need to make these unknown moments happen more often every day and as this happens the mind gets trained to live that way, walk that path, instead of the alternative from before where your train-wreck of a mind would go off the tracks at every little thing.

Not everyone is a "thought-freak" and some folks are more visually minded. So if you're one of those visual people you might not even have the word repeating you might see it written out in type, some kinda font. So the word has taken on a physical form in your mind's eye. It's like an item and that item is sitting with you in your meditation space right there in the room with you.

For me, my meditation game was already strong. I only started doing the mantra meditation technique just as a test to see if it really worked, and, all my favorite celebrities and comedians were doing it, so that sorta had an impact on me wanting to figure it out. At first I had some resistance because it wasn't as strict as my regular meditation routine. Eventually this T.M. shit became more than I could have dreamed of and now I do this every morning and sometimes at night anywhere from twenty minutes to an hour.

I made a meditation journal and I documented what happened during each session for the thirty days. I did those so I could look back and have some statistics to reference when explaining this to other people.

A little personal note from my own experience was that about halfway through the experiment my mantra started to take another form. So I was saying the word over and over to myself in my mind and eventually I began to just picture the word as I had drawn it out on paper one day in a sort of graffiti style.

That graffiti image sat with me in my mind as I meditated for a few days then it was as if the corners of the paper started to fold over from the top left corner to the bottom right corner and the top right corner folded to meet the bottom left corner in the middle. Imagine if you will, that the back side of the paper was all black, so now that the front was folded over I can't even see the graffiti anymore. What was left was just a sort of skewed rectangle, black in color. This sharp little item began to zip all around me. Just the one at first, then two appeared, and three and four... until there were hundreds and then thousands of them darting all around me creating a sphere, a bubble around my body. And hey, just keep in mind I am only seeing this inside my mine with my eyes closed as I sat there. Rather than reading the mantra with alphabet letters, words, speaking sounds, it had embodied a physical shape. Each little piece darting around was as if I was saying the word, they were representative of each time it was being said.

So that was just one example of how your mantra can shift and change. This changed mantra happened for several sessions where I would start out with the word and watch it fold in on itself until it became something smaller and more symbol-like. If I had to draw it out it would be a geometric rhombus shape. The mantra returned to being just a graffiti image in later sessions and so far it has not shifted away again.

I just wanna cycle back to something I said earlier about how eventually you feel like you need an upgrade, and that is sorta where the shadiness to this comes into play. It's not that you really need an upgrade, it's more that you were living your life in a deficit before where you were in the negative and now by pulling yourself up to the level or to the zero-zone made that trip going upwards feel like a "high". Now that you're at the level it starts to get boring and you aren't feeling that high anymore and that's pretty much because you're back to being normal, and normal is boring, normal sucks, right?

So this is where people get caught-up in needing something more once they have reached that plateau and this is where the T.M. people start rubbing their hands together with dollar signs in their eyes and they can't help but tell you that of course there is a next level! Just pay the price and come learn some new breathing techniques. Those breathing techniques will give you that high until they become normalized and then what? Then you can keep chasing the high or you can learn to live with what you have.

T.M. is a heavily guarded secret online! What ended up happening with me was that I found someone who took the course and they told me how to do it. But that's not really the same as learning this from the professionals.

Anyone who is seriously interested in this style of meditation should contact your local T.M. center and book an appointment with them because they are far better at explaining this than I am with my internet research.

KUNDALINI MEDITATION

Okay, this is a weird one right? How the fuck do you even pronounce that word? Koon-Dah-Lee-Nee. This is another Sanskrit word, it's a feminine adjective that means either circular or coiled and it's often described simply as "The Coiled One" which is also represented as two snakes coiled at the base of your spine.

During this meditation the coiled up energy travels up your spine through a system called the Chakras. Okay, wait, Chakras? We're getting a little too hippie dippie here right? Well, maybe.

Let's look at the earth. For sure we know about something called the "Ley Lines" of the earth. These are energy lines that travel around the planet and the body has similar energy lines, scientifically proven. These energy lines in our bodies do end though, and these endpoints are called "Nadi Points". When two of these energy lines intersect to make a cross, this is where a Chakra appears. You might have seen Chakras in pictures before and there are seven or eight of them going up your spine but there are also more them going through your arms and legs too, but we don't talk about those ones very often. Now that that's outta the way let's get back to the snakes!

The two coiled up snakes travel up the spine through the Chakras reaching the top of your head and then go back down again, giving the meditator an incredible sense of energy transmission that sometimes can result in tingling sensations up the spine, panic attacks, and even seizures in some cases.

I'm sure you've all seen like the scepter or staff with two snakes coiled around it with their heads meeting at the top? Probably on a doctor's prescription pad or part of the logo on a doctor's office? This image is directly linked to the Kundalini snakes, kinda like an homage to the old more mystical way of doing things, and, health in general.

Kundalini is a feminine energy. That's not to say that if you're a dude you have a woman's energy inside you this is simply a way of describing a duality of energy. It could be different words like black and white, up and down, good or bad and for the nerds out there ones and zeros!

You may have heard about Kundalini Yoga where some people experience little trips similar to LSD or Shrooms. In Kundalini yoga there is a lot of breath-work. It involves constricted and fast breathing.

With the meditation session it begins with a walking breath-work with something like four steps per breath. After this you do a seated breath-work such as the breath-of-fire technique which is made up of short bursts of air similar to like when a lady is giving birth (Hooo-Hooo! - Haaaaaaaahhh! This is followed by visualization and breath-work together where you start to visualize the two coiled serpents at the base of your own spine, which represent the built-up energy that is to be released.

I'll just note here the only reason they say it's made of snakes is because when the energy rises and falls it sort of feels like it would maybe be snakes. You could replace snakes with ropes or strings if that makes you feel more at ease.

Next you envision this energy, sort of in the form of these two serpents traveling up your spine to the top of your head and then leading back down. So yeah, if this is your jam, this is your cup of tea, this is your thing, then keep on doing it!

If doing breathing shit like this is in fact your jam you might like something called "Holotropic Breathing" made famous by Wim Hof among a few others in the world of breath-work. In holotropic breathing you sit with a spotter (yeah man, breathing can get dangerous!) because people sometimes get asphyxiated and they can pass out, fall over and bang their head. Some people break out into tears and some go into little mini seizures of convulsive fits. And now that I've painted such a beautiful picture of how this can fuck you up let me explain what it really does for most people.

Most folks just lay there and do this breathing, it's something like ten really fast breaths followed by four really slow breaths. The four slow breaths should take just as long to do as the ten fast breaths. Do this repeatedly for about ten minutes and your brain breaks. You escape from this world as it all just melts away and you're transported on a psychedelic journey into the depths of your own mind. This is one hundred percent safe and one hundred percent legal. Nobody can tell you how to breathe in the comfort of your own home.

I have done this myself just lying in bed in the dark and I did this without a spotter because I'm just hardcore like that. After about ten minutes of breathing in this way, all that I could see was the darkness, that sort of dark you get from eyelids. Then it went even darker, a pitch black!

The black began to bubble as if someone had put a flame behind a piece of black nylon fabric and holes were melting into the fabric. Behind these holes I found myself being pulled along on a track through a jungle scene of trees, giant leaves and a bright blue sky. The world of my bedroom did not exist as I was fully immersed in this new realm, this new state of consciousness. Popular topics such as connectivity were communicated to me while the overall feeling was similar to the epiphanies one gets during an LSD experience. A profound knowledge was entering into me and it was not with words like "Hey, this is how this or that works in life" it was more of an instant knowing. The information was being sent over sort of like how a computer file gets downloaded and it is all there at once. Imagine if your brain worked like a computer where instead of slowly learning things all the information was just suddenly there. At this point I opened up my eyes to see that I was still in my bed and when I closed my eyes there was only darkness. If you attempt this at home please involve another person you trust to remain quiet and calm during the situation.

THE MOMENT MEDITATION

I know at some point in life you've sat at a traffic light where the light has turned green but you didn't see that shit. Maybe you were rockin out to your favorite tune or deep in some introspective thought but you just sat there like a dummy until the angry fucks behind you started layin on their horns.

This is sort of where we are going with the moment meditation, although without the spaced-out aspect. We want to be in that empty vacuum of space but also have our two feet planted in this world, rooted deep into the earth. The key is that we are not being dominated by our thoughts.

When I first learned about The Moment Meditation it was presented as one of the most advanced techniques you can only get to after you have mastered one of these other methods. I did it the first try! I say, shoot for the stars! You can try doing this right now, put the book down, and just simply follow your breath for about three breath cycles. See how easy that was? It's so easy and quick and simple that it's the best way to ensure meditation makes its way into your daily life throughout the day and not just regulated to the set session times you have put aside.

This is sort of like a quick moment to moment drop-out. There is nothing involved for this. It is so simple as there are no timers or bells or gongs. There's nothing to do with your mind. There's no mantras to repeat and no meditation music needed. But when the fuck would anyone do this? To give some examples: when you are out in public perhaps standing in lines like at grocery or corner stores, banks, sitting at a gas station waiting for a pump to free-up. These are great chances to drop-out and enter a brief meditative state rather than being bombarded by the marketing of the colors on the wall, colors of the packaging, the bright fluorescent lights and all that bullshit that's been designed to mess with your subconscious to make you want to do some impulse buys near the checkouts. This little drop-out allows you to skip right over all of that nonsense and get right to where you want to be, at the till, paying your hard earned money, for some food, or gas or some banking, or whatever the fuck you're there for.

Pretty much any time where you are waiting for someone or something to happen the Moment Meditation comes into play. By bringing meditation out into the world and into your daily life routine you will start to notice that you are more clam when things do not go your way. Say for example you're doing your groceries and you happened to have chosen the shortest line there is and some older person ahead of you cannot figure out their pin number on the card. Maybe they are trying to redeem several hundred coupons that each need to be entered one at a time. Perhaps they wanna pay with a check and nobody has used checks since the 1980's so the clerk needs to call in a manager for approval.

Your wisely chosen shortest lineup has become a nightmare of waiting as you stand ogling angrily at them for taking so long. Sure you could read some trashy gossip paper or fidget around looking at the bullshit items around you and maybe pick one or two of them up to add to your cart, or gaze longingly at your cell phone, but what are you really doing? All you're doing is trying to make the time pass by either putting garbage into your mind or adding garbage into your cart. This right here my friends is the perfect time to drop-out and enter The Moment Meditation. That will keep your blood pressure lower, your cortisol levels low resulting in less insulin spikes which in the end leads to a healthier overall life.

Another example would be your lunch break, rather than scrolling endlessly through social media, take a moment, and drop-out. Close your eyes and follow three or more breath cycles without any other sensory inputs other than the chair under your ass!

MY PERSONAL MEDITATION AND HOW IT HAS GROWN

My seating of choice is always full lotus. I know, I know, I use all these weird words! What the fuck is a lotus anyways? It's a flower, that's all, and when you cross your legs into a pretzel shape it kinda looks like lotus leaves I guess. Most people cannot do a full lotus so they do a half lotus.

Okay so to put it plainly my legs are crossed, my back is straight, my neck is straight, my head is gazing forward and my eyes are closed. My arms go out to rest on my knees and at first palms are clutching onto the knee caps as I sway my torso around in large circles that get smaller and smaller until I arrive at my core center and stop once there.

Starting from the base-up with a sort of kegel energy (I really shouldn't get into what a kegel is, but it's when women do like vagina flexes to strengthen the vaginal walls and when dudes do that dick-flex that makes your bonner move; those are called kegels! And that is in fact a real exercise that people do and you would flex and hold). So yeah, this kegel energy is sort of drawing upwards from the base of the spine to the tip of the head. My arms are out and resting on knees with my palms facing up at this point or with the index fingers touching the thumbs kinda making that hand sign for "OK", the arms being out like that helps to stabilize the back from swaying a round. Occasionally I will sit with my hands in the Zazen position with the left hand cradled under the right hand and the two thumbs touching creating that sort of egg shape in the open space between them. I find that there is a subtle energy force at play with the hand placements, but, maybe I'm just making that up.

The palms up tend to draw in energy while the closed circuit of the thumb and fingers seem to keep it circulating within the body. Often when the meditation is drawing to an end I will keep one hand in the closed circuit with the other hand lifted and the palm pointing outward into the room as if I were about to wave at someone. This allows any excess energy to be released into the room. Excess energies can be just as damaging as a lack of energies.

Sometimes we have a lot of pressure in our temples as thoughts seem to hover around in this area. Our jaws get clenched and a pressure is built up. By opening the jaw loosely and allowing it to rest open easily, softy, and this pressure is often released. To go further into this I like to try and focus all of my attention to the top of my head as if I were trying to look out through my crown up at the stars above. By practicing this it allows my mind and thoughts to gravitate upwards instead of weighing down in the two side temple areas and I feel a pressure is released, a weight has been lifted.

I regularly do constricted nasal breathing too. This method will be further explained in the techniques section later on. I breathe deep into my belly and then followed by the lungs, the belly breathing uses the diaphragm (like with singing) and I empty all of the air, all the way out until there is none left. I breathe long slow breaths all the way in. The use of the constricted nasal breathing allows for the long slow breathing to take place at a regular pace without feeling like you are depleted of oxygen and struggle to gasp for air like you were drowning.

I am watching the thoughts float by and looking at them as foreign objects not of my own creation. I did not make these they are just there. It's kind of like, you can run to the window to watch every car that drives down the road or you can sit on the couch. You can still hear them in the background, you know they are there, but you do not have to go look at them and study what make and models they are. You definitely do not run out into the street and jump into those cars and start driving them. If the road is a highway you do not get angry about how fast they were going like "Arrrrgh! How dare they go so fast on this highway? Arrrgh!" and now you are all caught-up in the anger of it all, am I right?

So what do I do when the thoughts start to flood in too much, too fast and too frequent? I return to the breath. If I catch myself in a thought loop I go back to the breath. Breathe in, out, in, out. Always taking note of the sound of the breath and how it reminds me of the ocean waves noting the physical sensations in my body as I breathe.

This is a discipline. It is something you do every day at the same time each day for the same amount of time. A routine. Repetition creates a hypnosis of sorts and this comes from things like chanting, reciting mantras and even the breathing. It puts the body into a trance-like state and in this state we are able to see life more clearly for what it is and work through our own melodramas.

But wholly fuck, let me tell ya! Some days none of this shit is happenin! I sit there and it's already too late as the ol' thought-train has left the station and it's full speed ahead!

So now what? What do you do? You do nothing. You get up and you go about your day. Do not beat yourself up over it man, I mean, this shit happens sometimes. Not getting angry at yourself is really the key to all of this.

Maybe you're sitting there and you're doing real well and those thoughts are just floating by and then you have focused on one of them and you are going down a rabbit hole of thoughts and you are not even noticing it. When and if you do notice it try not to be annoyed with yourself. Your inner voice is very important as it creates the outer-you. If you are trying to meditate yourself into a better life then there is no point in yelling at yourself while doing it.

When I first started this shit it was only to get away from my brother and sister while on vacation. I was probably only nine years old. We all kept fuckin nagging at each other until one day I climbed up on a big rock, crossed my legs and closed my eyes. That was the end of all our bickering!

But like hey man, I had no idea what I was doing, this was just some shit I had seen on martial arts movies and with Master Splinter on Ninja Turtles! I meditated off and on throughout my life. It was a lot more of the 'off' through my twenties during those party-years of being in a band.

So yeah, even as a child all I knew was to sit with your eyes closed and that would be enough, until I learned about following the breathing. Following the breath worked a little better as having something to follow, it was something to do while sitting there and it's the best thing to do because it's always there. Like, you don't need any special music or beads or anything. Got some thoughts happenin? Follow the breath!

Following the breath worked for the most part until recently when I started trying out these Transcendental mantra meditations. And that shit was like, a fuckin game changer!

So the new and improved, adapted from what I've learned, version of my meditation goes like this:

I start out seated in either full or half lotus. I sway around to give the back a little stretch and find the center. Eyes are closed. And I do this constricted nasal breathing like before and now instead of worrying about my breath I just repeat the mantra to myself. RaMaSa. This thing has been repeated thousands of times today. The reason why I like this better is because it has no meaning. The breath is still breathing and when I focus on my breath all sorts of images come into my mind related to breathing, from my chest rising and falling to the bronchial tubes in my lungs. The mantra, RaMaSa, is just a meaningless word that allows me to come back to something that won't cause any more extra thought streams. But like I'm not super strict about this either so I incorporate different things each time and switch some things around.

The meditation needs to be a part of your routine, but the meditation itself doesn't need to be exactly the same every day. So, sometimes I sit with my hands on my kneecaps, sometimes palms are up, sometimes making the "OK" sign with finger and thumb, sometimes they are fists and sometimes one hand is cradled in the other hand. Some mornings I do twenty minutes and sometimes it's thirty minutes and then sometimes it's a full hour.

You see, what I have done is incorporate several techniques into one master technique that is currently working for me. I understand that someday it might not work anymore and that I will always need to keep researching and learning and developing new techniques. If I had any advice for y'all just startin out, I'd say just do what feels right and let the rest fall into place and don't believe all the churchy woo woo shit about this stuff because it's mostly all bullshit. So take what you need and go and don't look back, and don't over-think the process. The hardest part is starting.

So that's it for my personal meditation tactics and a short history of why I started and all that.

THE LOVING KINDNESS MEDITATION

So far all of these techniques have been quite self-involved where we are working on ourselves to be the best that we can be! I mean we are already pretty fuckin cool and it never hurts to get a little cooler! This next shit, The Loving Kindness meditation is a bit different though as it starts to deal with some outside shit. It deals with some of the people and events outside of your control.

This technique helps build empathy toward others to create positive relationships. Now the word relationship don't mean you and a woman, or you and a man, it could be with anyone from a boss to a work partner. This technique comes from a Buddhist tradition that's name translates to "Loving Kindness". This is where the person practicing focuses on the good things in other people and in life in general and having everyone taken care of.

Doing these Loving Kindness exercises increases our abilities to empathize with other people. So y'all just put this house together and the inspector comes along and starts picking it all apart so you're gonna be set back by a few more weeks of work to do! Loving Kindness, allows you to see that motherfucker is just doing his damn job. You start to see things like the fact that he also has a boss to answer to, and if he's already that much of a prick, you can guarantee his boss is an even bigger prick! So have some compassion for the dude!

There's some bullshit sounding stuff coming up but we just gotta get through a little bit of this shit, okay folks? So when you practice the Loving Kindness meditation you start to feel compassion, you feel empathy towards others. You start to notice facial features and expressions in a subtle way that helps you understand where someone is at, mentally and emotionally, so that you don't say the wrong things to make that person fly off the hinges!

What happens is that you start to have a better relationship with yourself. This might be things like accepting yourself for who you are, accepting all your faults, accepting social support from others, I know that's a hard one to let in sometimes, admitting that we need some help is often hard and then this starts to happen outwardly too having positive relationships with others. You start to feel competent about your own life and your ways of thinking, the way you master your environment and you have a purpose in life and it keeps you from acting egotistically.

A study that was published showed that even just a few minutes of this technique each day will greatly increase your social connection and create a more positive interaction with others.

So yeah, if you're a big fuckin loser, if you ain't got no friends and all you do is stay inside all the time and you won't even try to make any friends then this technique is for you. This is what burns the idea into your head that you might actually be cool. You get the sensation that you might actually have something worth saying and sharing with the world. This technique builds up your confidence and forces you to get out there and get social!

Examples of Loving Kindness meditation are easiest when they are guided meditations that you listen to as they kinda give you some shit to think about while you're sittin there.

So here is an example of one of those guided meditations led by a lady named Pema Chodron who is like one of the main people who bring this technique to the public. There won't be any more 'fuck words' in this next little section but I'm sure y'all can get through it!

Transcription of Pema Chodron:

"During this meditation you are encouraged to sit as you would in other meditations. Legs crossed, spine is straight, arms either zazen (folded in front with one hand cradled in the other) or out resting on your knees with whatever mudra (Spiritual hand gang sign) that suits you.

Keep your chest and heart space wide open, no hunching over. Eyes are open and gazing at the floor about three or four feet in front of you. You become aware of your ordinary breath as it goes out and in, with more emphasis on the outward breath, expanding and dissolving into the space around you.

You relax outward with the breath. Without any struggle you remain present with your breath as it expands outward and you keep coming back to this breath, over and over again. In a simple and relaxed way, you keep coming back to the breath as thoughts arise in your mind, coming and coming, as soon as you notice them, acknowledge them in a relaxed an non-judgmental way by saying to yourself "Ahh.. Thinking" or "Ahh... thoughts" and "Ahh... emotions" and then you come back to the out-breath, relaxing outwardly with your out-breath.

Thoughts and emotions can appear solid and tangible yet when you notice them, equate them to the same as seeing clouds in the sky, you do not try to climb into the air to grab and hold every cloud that floats by, and so you do not try to latch onto any emotions, feelings or thoughts that are floating by. Instead you allow them to dissolve back into the sky, always regarding your thoughts as clouds in a vast sky-space.

When your body starts to hurt, back pain or hips or legs, try and stay with it for as long as you can but do not struggle. Once it gets to a point of total discomfort you may take a resting posture such as putting up your knees and holding on to them, or a child's pose, a back stretch forward or a side stretch until you are ready to return to the seated posture, without any struggle.

Sometimes the instruction "touch and go" helps. In your mind's eye, reach out with your finger and touch the breath, and let it go. Touch the thoughts and watch them dissipate as if you were popping a floating soap bubble. This is not a process of getting rid of your thoughts but overtime you will begin to see their transparency and how they do not hold any power over you simply because they exist. Seeing that they are not all that solid, do not struggle against them, being relaxed, just touch them and let them go. Relaxing the mind, relaxing the body, touch and go.

Always returning to the out-breath. Keeping in mind the gentleness, there is nothing harsh in this meditation technique, you do not whip about in a panic or a frenzy to stop intrusive thoughts, you simply allow them to float, gently, softly, no matter how harsh the content of the thoughts or feelings, always returning to the out-breath. No matter what the content, be it harsh or not, you can always just say "Ahh... thinking" and never taking it too serious, keeping a light humor to it with almost a chuckle "Hehe... thinking" or "Hehe... Oh those silly thoughts!"

The point is to cultivate unlimited friendliness with your own thoughts or emotions so that they are not the enemy but a friendly gift that you do not have to accept. You can say thank you for the gift and hide it away on a shelf never to be opened".

So yeah, what is happening here, on the brain-wash level, is that you're always focusing on the out-breath, outwardly, looking to the external and that shit starts to reflect back through your daily life. You start to grow and reshape your minds to be more compassionate outwardly. When the mind changes the body follows suit and then the outside environment follows.

We stop thinkin about ourselves as bein isolated or separated from the group. We start to feel connected! The goal isn't to stop thinking. The goal is to realize that your thoughts aren't real, they aren't a thing, there's no substance to them. Any thought or emotion can be dissolved simply by touching it.

Transcription of Sharon Salzberg:

"Loving Kindness is meant to be done in the most easiest way possible. Use phrases that are personally meaningful, beginning with oneself. May I be free from danger, inner danger like the force of certain mind states and outer danger. May I know safety, mental happiness, physical happiness, ease of wellbeing, to not have to struggle day by day with family and livelihood issues.

Use any phrases that are powerful for you, they need to be meaningful not just in a temporary way, but in a profound way that you wish for yourself and for others. Do not struggle to get a certain kind of feeling, let your mind rest in the phrases, you can be aware of the phrases with the breath, or just focusing on the phrases alone.

Feelings will come and go, some extraordinary, some are very dry or ordinary, mechanical. It doesn't mean that it's not working, what is important is to do it from that intention in the mind and that is what will produce the effect of the free flow of loving kindness.

Repeating the loving phrases allows your mind to begin to associate them with your daily life. For example, you have been doing the phrases daily and you stub your toe, bang your elbow and knock a jug of water onto the floor and you might catch yourself saying things like – Oh you're such a klutz! But I love you!

The next step is sending loving kindness to neutral people, those you might have met but have no judgments about them and to those we have difficulty with, like our enemies! With phrases such as "This person wants to be happy just as I want to be happy".

Sending loving kindness to our enemies can be difficult, sending unconditional love and affection that may not be reciprocated because of their conditions, the condition is that they have an issue with you. When your own strong feelings or anger begin to arise about this person allow those thoughts to dissolve and try again later, or attempt this meditation, these phrases, with another person who is a lesser enemy.

There comes a time when you may be sending loving kindness to this evil person and they start to become better and more happy and you may realize you don't want them to be happy, they are your enemy, right? It is at this point that you look within, and find that once your enemies are feeling better they won't necessarily be your enemy anymore, and you can meet on a common ground".

Okay, let's try to unpack this bag of bullshit. How the fuck does being nice with words fix your life, exactly? Well, let's flash back to you sitting in traffic again, because it's easy to picture and we all do it so often. And I mean, all this meditation stuff runs off experience. It's like the first time you tried to use a hammer compared to the thousandth time you swung a hammer. You got better at it. Your aim improved. You don't even need to look anymore it just kinda hits the nails almost by itself.

So you're sitting in traffic and some ass-wipe cuts you off nearly causing an accident and there it is; the anger, the pain, the hurt, the distraught feelings and now you're projecting the future of what could have happened, but didn't!

In your mind's eye you reach your finger out and you touch those emotions and poof! They are all gone! Dissolved. And then instead of freaking out for the next half hour to an hour with your heart pumping and your adrenaline rushing and your cortisol levels maxed out, instead you just drive calmly home not even thinking about what just happened. Through the loving kindness practice you have been able to leave all that anger and fear back at that last traffic light stop.

Personally, for me, I haven't tried this method very much, probably because I'm too self-involved and hung up on my own inner workings that

I don't really focus too much on the external world. I believe that true change comes from within. By starting on myself deep inside I can make those changes and they can be reflected through my home and my lifestyle.

This leads as an example to those around me like my friends and my family. Family is always watching, those little nieces and nephews growing up, even when you think they aren't watching you are paying close attention to all of this shit! So be prepared for that!

The positive thing I have noticed from doing the few Loving Kindness meditations that I have done is that I don't get so heated anymore, I don't get all riled up from things that used to get me steamed. There are certain family members that are a constant challenge for this as they try their hardest to get me all worked up and angry. However, now that their little jabs no longer work they tend to leave me alone and we can all laugh at humorous things about myself or about my lifestyle that used to make me angry.

There are some other aspects of my life where people or situations would get a rise out of me and those have all now gone away, and those people just leave me alone.

But shit, a situation itself cannot go around trying to fuck people over, but what has happened is that I am no longer gravitated to those situations or the people involved with them and those people are not gravitating toward me anymore.

This can definitely be a bit lonely at first and shit man, you might even try to break out of it and get some attention by going down those old roads again. If it happens it happens, whatever, but I mean, try not to do that! We gotta slowly start to integrate and allow for that integration to happen and that ain't happening if we keep goin down those same old roads.

New people and new situations that are more in harmony with our own new way of looking at things will start to become attracted to us and us to them. We have to allow this to happen and not block these people out, so we need to keep an open mind.

Like, maybe you always thought a potluck dinner with a bunch of local community members was a stupid idea and you need to ask yourself a question: How has that been working for you? Open up, try some potluck! Have some new meals you never had before and before you know it you've gone and made a new friend, that may just need some work done on their house and you're just the person to do it!

ZEN MEDITATION

This method is also known as Zazen which in some schools of thought is also used to describe the seated posture that is done in this meditation. As some of you may have even heard it said before "They were sitting Zazen on the floor".

This is where this shit gets a little more strict and demanding of how you do it.

Zen meditation is done in a quiet place where you can sit without any distractions, I mean that right there is some bullshit, fuck that noise! For example the T.M. meditation I do is done when there are road crews working on the sidewalk outside of my own bedroom window. I feel that having something there like a regulation or a rule is just another thing to get in the way of you maybe not doing it. Ya know? It's like, "Oh well, I couldn't get to a quiet place today so I guess I just won't even meditate!"

According to the rules the room should be neither too dark nor too bright, warm in the winter and cool in the summer. The sitting place should be neat and clean. When possible place an offering of flowers on the altar and burn some incense. Pictures of Buddhas, Gurus or statues of Gods or Goddess can be placed in the room on an alter. And again I just wanna say this already has too many rules and blockages to prevent you from meditating because if you can learn to meditate with the noise and the dirt in a room free of incense and altars with statues, you can meditate anywhere in the world!

The rules say that you need a good amount of sleep and you should not be physically exhausted, so that right there cuts out after work meditations. Before sitting down eat a moderate meal and avoid alcohol, drugs or stimulants. So basically you gotta do this after eating, but before any coffee. Wash your face and feet so that you feel refreshed. So I guess that means have a shower right after you eat breakfast, but before your coffee.

Your clothes man, they can't be too crazy! Nothing too expensive either! Try to avoid heavy clothes that might weigh your shoulders down too much. Your clothing should be loose fitting but neat in appearance, like, ironed or pressed.

When it's time to sit down you fold your legs up like a pretzel or a half pretzel, which they call Lotus or Half Lotus. If your fucking knees are up higher than your hips, that shit ain't right, sit your ass on a pillow or a cushion until your hips are up higher than your knees, it might take quite a few pillows for different people's body types.

Now put your hands with the palms facing up, resting on your knees and start to sway the upper half of your body from left to right, just a few times. Now sway from front to back and stretch out your waist and hip muscles, but without moving your hips at all. The sways should start out wide and get smaller and smaller until they end with your upper half being perfectly centered.

Next place your hands gently in your laps in front of you with your left hand on top and right hand on the bottom with both thumbs touching so that the space that's left open kinda has an egg shape to it.

Your mouth should be closed but with your tongue pressed up on the roof of your mouth inside.

Keep your eyes slightly open and looking down about a meter in front of you and at a forty five degree angle. Now don't focus on anything in particular but just let everything have its place in your field of vision. If your eyes are closed you might fall into a state of drowsiness, daydreaming or even sleep.

Inhale and exhale a full deep breath through the mouth, smoothly and slowly. In order to squeeze all the air from your lungs use the diaphragm, or the belly, like with singing. Close your mouth and keep breathing naturally through your nose. Man, I'm tellin ya, there are way too many steps to this nonsense so far, it had better pay off in the end! Right?

Keep breathing through the nose on a natural rhythm, don't try to control your breathing. Let the breathing come and go as natural as possible while keeping those long and full deep breaths. But, if they happen, let them happen; let short be short and long be long, no struggle here. But try not to make any noise by breathing heavily.

You don't need to think about any certain object or ideas or people or anything like that and you don't need to control your thoughts at all. When you keep the right posture and your breathing settles down your mind, you will naturally become more calm and tranquil. But, when thoughts do start poppin off do not get caught up in them and don't struggle with them.

Don't try to pursue them and don't try to escape from them either. Just leave the thoughts alone allowing them to come and go away freely on their own. The essential key to doing Zen meditation is to become alert and aware of any distractions or even any dullness as soon as it happens, and then, return to the posture, moment by moment.

When it's time to get up, you bow, place your hands palms up on your thighs, sway your body a few times once again in each direction, starting off slowly and getting more aggressive and extensive. Take one deep breath. Exhale. Unfold your legs gently, don't let them slingshot out, and begin to move very slowly. Never stand up too quickly.

MINDFULNESS MEDITATION

Mindfulness helps us put some space between ourselves and our reactions and it breaks down all the bullshit programming that's been built up over our lives, our conditioned responses.

Here is how you can tune into some mindfulness during the day.

Set aside some time. You don't need a special meditation cushion or a magical bench or any sort of special gear or clothes to access your own mindfulness skills, but you do need to set aside some time and space, this is probably the hardest part of any meditations. I do have the time and space set aside and there are mornings when I just can't do it. It's already too late as I said earlier the "Thought-Train" has left the station, full steam ahead! And in those times it's important not to try and fight the mind with more mind!

Observe the present moment as it is. The goal of mindfulness is not making your stupid mind shut the fuck up and it's not to get into a state of never-ending calm. The goal is simple, we're trying to just pay attention to the present moment, right here, right now, without any judgment. That means the moment could be good or the moment could be bad, but either way, you just tune into that moment and recognize it without trying to push it away or be distracted from it. This is easier said than done of course.

Let your judgment roll by! Whenever we notice judgments during this time just make a mental note, like "Ahh... judgment" and let that shit roll on by!

Return to observing the present moment as it is. Our minds get carried away in thoughts. That is why mindfulness is the practice of returning, again and again, to the present moment. Right here, right now! What's that? Dropped an auger on your toe? Tough shit, deal with it, right here, right now!

Be kind to your mind. Don't judge yourself for whatever the thoughts are that pop up, just practice recognizing them when your mind has wandered off and gently bring it back to the present moment. Right here, right now!

And that's it. That's all there is to this method of mindfulness meditation, it's quite simple, but not all that easy to do. If you keep doing it you'll see the results.

A VERY BASIC MEDITATION TECHNIQUE

Now that we're at the end of this segment I'll give y'all a little meditation demonstration, this is a super easy and relaxed method that you can try, this one doesn't have any special names attached to it, it doesn't come from thousands of years of doing it this way, this is just a simple and easy to do method that anyone can do at nearly anytime.

This meditation focuses on your breath again. There is nothing special about your breath but the physical sensation of breathing is always there and you can use the breath as an anchor to hold you to the present moment. Right here, right now!

Throughout this practice you might get all caught up in some thoughts, emotions, or even sounds – wherever your damn mind goes, simply come back again to the next breath, right here, right now.

If you only come back once that's okay too!

It may help to have someone read this to you for the first few times until it sticks.

Sit comfortably. Find someplace that gives you a stable and solid comfortable seat where you are less likely to slouch or have a curved lower back.

Notice what your legs are doing. If you're on a cushion cross your legs comfortably in front of you, do a pretzel if that's your thing, if not just do a regular crossed legs, whatever is the most comfortable to you. Or use a chair, and if you're on a chair just make sure the bottoms of your feet are flat on the floor.

Straighten your upper body. Don't stiffen your body, you're not a meditation robot here. Your spine has its natural curve so let that be as it is.

Notice what the fuck your arms are doing. Keep your upper arms parallel to your upper body. Rest your palms on your legs wherever it feels the most relaxed for you, each person is different.

Soften your gaze. Drop your chin a little and let your gaze fall gently downward. It's not required that you close your eyes. You can simply let what appears before your eyes to be there without really focusing on it, like, you don't need to struggle to see a chair in the room when a fuzzy out of focus chair will work the same. But then like, even if there is a chair, or whatever it is, don't be tryin to focus on that shit at all and if it's there just let it be there but don't try and look at it directly. Just keep everything in that same kinda fuzzy zone like when you see shit through your peripheral vision.

Feel your breath. Bring your attention to the physical sensation of your breathing. Feel the air moving through your nose or mouth, feel the rising and falling of your belly and your lungs.

Notice when your mind wanders away from the breath. Eventually your attention will leave the breathing and start to wander off to other places. That's okay. There is no need to block or eliminate your thinking. Whenever you do notice your mind wandering gently return to the breathing.

Be kind about your wandering mind. You might find your mind wandering the entire session. That shit is totally normal too! Instead of fighting with your thoughts just practice observing them without reacting. Just sit and pay attention. As hard as it is to maintain, that's all there really is. Come back to your breath over and over again, without any judgments or any expectations.

When you're ready, gently lift your gaze. If your eyes are closed, gently bat your eyelashes open. Take a moment and notice any sounds in the room, or outside the room. Take a good note of how your body feels and notice your immediate thoughts and emotions.

That's it! You've done it! Maybe you only lasted one minute or twenty minutes but either way you've done something. You've taken that first step forward into the world of being the best possible human you can be. Optimized!

BINAURAL BEATS

Is it the fast track? Or is it just cheating?

I went to a Shambhala meditation center a few times when I lived close to one up in the mountains of British Columbia. After the meditation was over we all gathered in the common room and kitchen area for tea and cookies. Since I was the fresh spirit on the scene I was being drilled by everyone about all the fucking bullshit I can't stand talkin about and I really felt like I was right back in a gossipy ol' church again. I did not enjoy the twenty-one questions game about where I am from, what I do in life for work and who I was related to. I managed to look beyond their inquisitive ways to talk about some of the shit I wanted to talk about, like meditation. I mean, here we all were at a meditation center and all they wanted to talk about was the weather and who slept with whom and what the next town election is going to mean. But like, I had questions, real questions! When I got into talking about binaural beats and how they catapult you about twenty minutes into a meditation state, these elder meditators got a little unsettled and they accused me of cheating and that I was not doing the work. One of them scoffed at me, got up and left the table. You see for some people meditation can be a lot of deep inner work on their psyches, a self-therapy of sorts and it doesn't need to be that way for everyone.

To interject in this story, here is another story!

A PARABLE OF THE BUDDHA

One sunny day the Buddha was walking along the water's edge when he came upon a monk deep in meditation. The monk, who saw the Buddha approaching jumped up to greet him and explained to the Buddha that he would sit and meditate for a thousand years if he had to until he could walk on the water over to that island in the distance. To this the Buddha said "Why? The ferry is only a nickel".

When I started doing the T.M. meditations, for the first thirty days there were construction crews directly outside my window with jack hammering sounds that would start at seven AM every morning and finish up at seven PM every night. It was a struggle trying to learn a new method with all that fucking noise out there! I now feel different about binaural beats as they do in fact get you "there" much quicker but I have learned to enjoy the process of getting there and not feeling the need for this electronic crutch.

There were times when early in the morning as it was nearing the designated meditation time that I would look around the room and I couldn't find my fucking headphones! So I did not meditate that day because I could not use the binaural beats. Today I meditate twice daily for the most part without using anything external. There are noises, roommates, kids upstairs and pets crawling all over me but I still manage to get through it. It is just as easy to do without anything else added to the process. The more layers we can peel away, the better. The more ways we can prevent ourselves from ever having an excuse to not meditate is only better for us in the end.

So what the fuck are binaural beats? I hope you're ready to get into some science!

This is quite simple actually. It goes back to the days of giant gongs, bells, singing bowls and anything else that causes a loud vibration. People of the past knew that all life is made of vibrations and that vibrations can affect and change and affect even other vibrations.

We take a 130hz frequency from the left and shoot it out into the middle of the room. We take a 40hz frequency from the right and aim it into the center of the room so that the two frequencies meet and clash in the middle. What happens is an entirely new frequency is created out nowhere as the two current frequencies cancel each other out. One frequency brings the other frequency up, while the other brings the other one down, resulting with the difference of the two frequencies left directly in the center, all the while the original two frequencies are still there.

In this example you shot a 130hz from the left and a 140hz from the right which leaves you with 10hz, the difference of the two. This magically created 10hz can only be heard by positioning yourself right in the middle of the room.

I know what you're thinking: How the fuck can you buy some giant-ass gongs and position them in the room, bang on them, run to the middle of the room and sit down quickly to meditate? The answer is so simple. You cannot.

Headphones. The 10hz frequency that will be vibrating inside your skull will be changing and affecting your own inner, organic vibrations. Sound frequencies are vibrations and have the power to alter other vibrations.

We have learned through quantum physics that most of the universe is either a particle or a wave, that is, a frequency that can affect us. They can change us, alter our moods by either bringing us up or bringing us down and they can also make us feel nauseous or sick but they can also heal us. This science, or this medicine really, is being used all over the world in healing centers in the form of sound-baths where the patient lays on the ground as they are washed over with different frequencies known to help heal and raise the patients vibrations.

Binaural beats have been studied for many years and there is a wealth of knowledge and samples available online for download from places like the Monroe Institute where a professor Robert Monroe was the first to start researching this phenomena of the mysterious third frequency that occurs.

When this frequency happens right in the center of your mind as you listen with headphones the left and right frequencies are still present and it sounds like a sort of wobbly "wah wah wah wah" sort of sound. This "wah wah wah wah" sound is the third frequency you are hearing deep inside your mind. This frequency is changing the vibrations of your mind. Since your mind is also broadcasting its own frequency back at your headphones, we would think that the headphones also would be altered, however, because they are coming from a machine, an audio file, that does not happen, as the headphones are like having a never-ending gong that never needs to be struck over and over again.

This also goes further to show how humans have the ability to affect each other from at a distance as each of our own frequencies are rolling out of us all the time and changing the world around us at a very subtle level, including other people around us.

And it's all available on Youtube, so that means you, that's right you, right now, can hop on the internet and listen to this shit in some headphones and it will boost you about twenty minutes deep into a meditation and you get to skip all the bullshit that usually happens at the beginning of your meditation sessions.

Each person will vibrate and gravitate to various different binaural beats. Each day it may be a different frequency. The videos are generally labeled along with a short description of what the frequencies have done for others in the past. For example you may find a file that says "Binaural Beats – Full body healing 3.5hz" and if that works for you, use it!

PHYSICAL TECHNIQUES

So this shit has sort of been covered already in the previous sections but let's just break it all down a bit more for you. I want you to get the best possible meditations happening once you begin the journey.

Most of this shit is done sitting down on the floor with your legs crossed or half crossed or whatever version of crossed works best for you. A full lotus is when you pull your left heel and foot up over the right leg and the right heel and foot up over the left leg to rest as the pressure from both keep your legs from flailing outward.

Man, I am tellin ya, this is kinda hard to do for most people and if this is not accessible to you only do one of the feet up over the opposite thigh and use whichever you want, it doesn't matter which foot goes first. I started doing this as a young child and so I can now do it without using my hands to help pull the feet into place. I used to always put the right foot first until I broke my metatarsals (toes) while skim-boarding one summer. After that the left foot had to go up first and the right foot second because there's just something slightly different about the pressure applied that was makin my broken toes hurt. By switching legs I found the pain to have subsided completely during the meditations.

When seated our base forms a triangle shape, bum and legs. By being down on the floor or close to the ground, or on the ground itself outdoors, we form a solid connection to the earth that grounds us energetically (hippie dippie woo woo) so that our sessions do not get too carried away, so that we do not drift into daydreaming.

A little more hippie dippie concept of the shape we form when seated cross legged is that we fit perfectly into the Merkabah spaceship for transcending into a 5D or a 6D reality, or even further. A Merkabah is essentially the shape of the Star of David, two three-sided triangular prisms placed one upside down inside the other. It is said that this is the shape of a metaphysical craft that carries consciousness, or the soul, from the earthly plane into the heavens. Yeah, I know right? Crayzeeee!

In the Shambhala Buddhist meditations it is okay to sit in a chair with your feet flat on the floor for a grounding connection with a straight back so that the spine, neck and head are pointed toward the heavens and with your hands resting on your lap in whichever mudra (spiritual hand gang sign) you desire to do, or simply with your palms facing upward (to receive the subtle hippie dippie woo woo energies falling from the sky).

Laying down to meditate is generally not practiced because everyone tends to fall asleep, daydream or become too drowsy to experience the full benefits of what is happening. Their minds become lazy and they do not get through any of the things that happen during meditation and they are not present in the moment. The breathing is also different when you are laying down. However there is an exception for every rule and so laying down can be done for Transcendental Meditation, where anything goes!

Some people like to stand when doing their meditations, such as with the "Moment Meditation" as you're in a lineup at a bank or a gas station as explained previously. It is not required to be seated although as explained previously the triangular base our legs form when crossed is a solid base and a solid connection to the earth for grounding.

Ojai Breathing Technique (Ooo-Jah-Eee), also called constricted nasal breathing, is done by holding your palm in front of your face and breathing as if you were trying to steam a mirror with your breath, like "HAAAAH". Then close your mouth and perform the same sort of breath only this time it will be more constricted and all the air comes out of your nose, like "HHHHMMMH". Then it's the same sensation on the inhale like "IIIMMMH" and out with another "HMMMMH". It is by doing this type of breathing that we are able to do long thirty second breaths in and out without fainting or gasping for more air.

Deep Belly Breathing, is when we breathe deep into the belly. Duhh? So on the inhale rather than swelling up our chests full of air we leave our chests as they are and we use the diaphragm muscle to push our belly's out filling that lower lung area full of air, on the exhale we use the belly muscle to pull the stomach back in which in turn pushes all of the air out. This is the method for breathing without using our lungs as much and relying heavily on the diaphragm (stomach muscles) instead.

Lung Yoga, is something that I came up with that I get my yogis to do at the beginning of every yoga class that I teach. So this really stretches out the lungs into the chambers that do not really get accessed on the regular. Our lungs are similar to the branches on a tree, we have the thick sturdy trunk and the branches get smaller and smaller as they develop further from the trunk. With lungs those small little stick branches do not really get accessed that much, or, they get little pockets of crud trapped in them as they are closed off nearer to the branch itself. So imagine you've been out in heavy traffic breathing in that pollution and some if it will get stuck in there so we really need to empty it all the way out.

Sitting in a comfortable cross legged position we get to empty out all of the air possible, really push-push-push all that air out. In fact, it may help to suck in the belly using the diaphragm to help push and empty the air out and it also helps to hold onto your knees and arch your back slightly to really squeeze any of the residual air left in there, get it all out! This next step must be avoided if you have blood pressure issues. Once you have all the air out we hold for the count of three seconds and then with ease and control we start to straighten our backs while simultaneously pushing our bellies out and this action naturally will fill the lungs back up with more air without relying on the lungs. We keep inhaling, inhaling, inhaling until there is absolutely no more space and we hold for the count of three. I like to repeat this process three times.

If during your meditation session you begin to feel as though your back is sore or you have become un-centered it's okay to hang onto your knees and give the torso soft gentle sways in a circular motion to the left and then to the right, starting with large circles and eventually having them get smaller and smaller until you have found your core center once more and, having stretched the back. Often times I will arch my back quite far and really lean back to give the mid-back zone a little loving stretch.

Binaural beats are definitely a technique, or more of a tool I suppose, to help us kick start our meditations. I suggest binaural beats for all beginners who want to see immediate results. However I do advise that they do not be used as a crutch for every meditation session because there becomes a dependency on them and we might not do our meditation if there are no binaural beats nearby. (This was especially true for myself and not having the beats handy became an excuse to not meditate).

MENTAL TECHNIQUES

So what the fuck are we doing the whole time that we sit there? Some say that all we are doing is sitting and that nothing else is needed. Some medical and scientific studies show otherwise; that by doing just a few small things we can improve our meditation sessions.

FOLLOW THE BREATH

The first thing you will hear about with meditation is people saying return to the breath like it's the best thing since sliced bread! The breath goes in, the breath goes out, what's the big deal? The deal is, that it's always there. It's always something you can focus on. It's easier than a mantra, it's easier than counting numbers, it's easier than, well than anything. I guess the next best thing would be to follow your eye blinks? Some people count beads, some do a mantra or a sing-songy chant and some stare at a picture of someone they believe to be an enlightened being.

So when the fuck are you supposed to follow or return to the breath? This is usually when you catch yourself thinking too much or going down a little rabbit hole of thoughts that have spiraled out of control and now you're a month ahead into the future thinking about what color socks you should wear at your cousins wedding. While the right color socks might mean a world of difference at a wedding, that's probably something you can worry about the day of, or the night before. Thoughts are normal and there is no stopping them. But, once you do catch yourself, you don't just say "Ahhh well shit, look at me I'm thinkin again!" and then continue on thinkin about the tux rental! No fuckin way man! You return to the breath. In,   and   out.

If you're busy thinkin about "in and out" then you're not projecting into the future at that wedding anymore are you? But even the words "in and out" have meaning and you might start to picture the words in your mind with each breath in and out. So instead of that it's more like you should embody the entire sensation of breathing as it happens. Feel the chest rise and fall. Feel the physical sensations of what "in and out" really means!

Every so often you will have surpassed the thoughts and surpassed the breathing and you will have entered into a total blissful state of relaxation without even knowing it. These spaces become more frequent as time goes on during your meditation practices day after day. The thing about these spaces is that you are not going to realize you are in them at the moment they are happening because realizing they are happening involves... more thinking! As soon as you realize "Oh hey, look at me mom! I'm meditating! I'm in the space!" well, that's just more thinking, and guess what? Yep, you guessed it! Time to return to the breath!

LETTING IT ALL GO

Sure, we've heard this said before, in movies and in songs, but how do you let it all go? What does that even mean?

Well, as we are sitting there watching the breath going in and out just try not to be perfect at everything. The point of letting it all go is not to get too hard on yourself and treat yourself with respect during these times. Afterward, when the meditation is done and you wanna call yourself all the names in the book, you go right ahead, but during meditation times we try to be nice to ourselves. Over time, this being kind to ourselves will start to leak out into our everyday lives.

What letting it all go means, is for sure letting go of your own self disapproval but it also means letting go of the thoughts too. And so, when we encounter a thought, we look at it, we watch it, we recognize it and we let it go. Some people like to give it a name and so when a thought happens they say "Ahh, thinking!" or "Ahh, thoughts" and if maybe they are not thoughts happening but instead emotions and feelings you have they are also labeled "Ahh, feelings" or more specific "Ahhh, feeling joyous!" or even feeling jealous or sad or whatever. And then you let them go and you move on into the next moment.

RETURN TO THE BREATH – START OVER!

Alright, sounds easy enough. So there you are, doin the damn thang; breath goes in and it goes out. Chest goes up and it goes back down. You're in a clear space and feeling good about it and then "WHAT'S FOR DINNER? WHAT AM I DOING TONIGHT? OH MY GOD I NEED A NEW TRUCK!" and so you tell yourself "Ahh, thinking" and there goes the dinner and you say "Ahh, doing" and tonight's plans fade away and you say "Ahh, the future" and you let that truck go off into the distance. None of these things were anything you could have dealt with right now in this very moment and that is the best time to let them all go and return to the breath.

ENTERING THE VOID

Now here is the shit that you've all heard about in meditation. This is what scares everyone and it's not even really a thing. People think that during meditation we need to completely shut the fuck up, in our heads. They think it's about entering some kinda void of nothingness. Well, here's the best part of that statement, even the nothing is a something once you label it. What is your concept of nothing? Would it be like the dark empty vacuum of outer space?

My idea of that nothing was more like a white overcast sky; no matter where you look it's all just a bright white glow where you're in this zone of emptiness with nothing to look at or think about or feel, but even all that is still something, it's a zone, it's a bright white glow!

The trap people fall into is becoming really good at creating this made-up zone in their minds and sitting down to meditate and they picture a white wall the whole time and never let any thoughts float by. That's not what we're tryin to do! It's not about forcing a made-up idea of what your version of the nothing is. Anyone can picture an overcast sky, you're probably doing it right now. It's easy, right? Yeah, so we don't ever force this on ourselves.

WARNING:
HIPPIE DIPPIE WOO WOO BULLSHIT STRAIGHT AHEAD

Use Caution. Travel at your own risk. A truckload of this bullshit spilled right out onto the road. You can try and get through it with everyone else or you can go around (Skip to the next Chapter!).

This next mental technique is not really a meditation but I feel it deserves a place within the context of what we are doing here inside our own minds, looking deeper within ourselves for answers to life's greatest questions and trying to calm the fuck down at the same time! I ain't even gonna say the name of this section cause I don't want y'all having any preconceived notions on what it's about until this segment is over.

This one needs some training ahead of time and you'll be getting to know yourself entirely. For this practice you just gotta lay down on your bed or sit up in a comfy chair. To start we begin at the bottom with our feet. Take your socks off and have a good look at those suckers! I mean really study them man! Look for wrinkles, hairs, crooked toe nails or anything unique about your own feet. As you stare at your feet, really begin to feel them, put all your focus and attention on them nasty-ass feet of yours!

So what are we lookin at here, we got some toes right? And the toes connect to the ball of your foot and it leads to an arch that connects to a heel. Maybe you have some flaky skin on your heel? Maybe your feet are extra soft and squishy? Or maybe they are all callused and hard as rock! Study every part of them. Wiggle your toes and notice how they move. Notice how your toe bones stretch out through the skin on top of your feet when your toes move.

Then we move upwards to the ankle. The ankle has little bones sticking out on the sides. Maybe there are some veins in there showing or maybe not. Wiggle your foot, watch it wiggle, note how the skin moves with it. Really begin to notice it though and really feel the sensations in your foot and ankle together now.

Yes! You feelin it? Once you have that down to the point that you could describe it to another person and they could visualize your foot and ankle, move further up the body.

Now there is a shin bone. Maybe it has scratches on it, maybe there is some hair or maybe its smooth and shaven. Flex your calf muscle and note how it looks and feels. And then, yep, you guessed it, we travel up the body some more to the knee. Bend that fuckin knee and extend that leg out long noticing every little thing about it; how the skin folks when the leg is extended or how it stretches when the knee is bent. Again, you keep moving upward through the body.

I think y'all are getting the point of what is happenin here by now! We continue doing this all the way up our bodies past the thighs into the groin, the stomach, the lower back (even though you cannot see your lower back try to visualize or go look in a mirror). We go all the way up our torsos and we stop. We start again at the fingertips by repeating what we have done for the toes with our fingers, hands, palms, wrists, forearms, elbows, biceps, shoulders, all the way up to the neck and finally our heads, our hair, our eyes, the blinking sensations, how our hair feels when it is touched or moved by something like a piece of fabric or even the wind.

Once we have fully surveyed our entire bodies and we have them committed to memory so that at any point you can instantly access what your left pinky finger looks and feels like when it is holding a cup of tea, then we are ready to start this technique.

For the process itself it's kinda easy to do. This is all going to be a process of visualization. Lay down in a bed or sit up in a chair with your feet on the ground. Close your eyes. Using our imaginations, in what we call the mind's eye, we can clearly see our feet, our ankles, shins, thighs and knees. Every part of us. In our minds eyes we can also see what these parts look like when they are moving, bending, twisting and doing things like walking or running, bending, crouching, breathing or anything we do in the real world.

This practice is best started in your own bedroom or someplace familiar. So there you are, with your eyes closed lying on your bed, for example. In your own mind you can see yourself in your bed. You know what the room looks like, you know what the bed looks and feels like and so you look around the room, eyes closed. There's your desk or lamp or whatever fuckin posters are on the walls. In your mind, get up out of the bed slowly. Visualize every little detail and feeling of what you are doing from the way the sheets move when you sit up to the way your legs feel when you swing them over the side of the bed. Get your feet planted on the floor and slowly stand up. Note the subtle things like the air in the room when you move about. Walk over to your desk or lamp or poster or some item in your room and study it, then study looking at other items using all the detail your imagination can muster up.

At this point your real body is in bed but in your imagination you've gotten up and moved around the room and you've begun to feel and sense things kinda like those vivid dreams that seem so real. The next step after you have been all around your room and inspected everything in great detail is to move out of the room. Head over to the door, reach out for it and open the door then exit the room. When you leave the room you'll see you are still in your own house or apartment or flat, and that nothing is different. You can travel down hallways into washrooms, into your siblings or flatmates rooms but try not go into places that you have never been in before if you have a flatmate that never lets you into their space it's best to respect their privacy.

Move through the common rooms that you normally move through in the run of a day. Explore everything. Open the fridge, look at the food, maybe even reach in and take a drink of something. Picture the flavor of that drink. It could be orange juice with a citrus tang that tingles the taste buds. Imagine even how it feels going down your throat and that slightly cold chill deep inside the belly.

Once you've been fully through your entire home and really explored every corner of it knowing it just as you do in waking life, then, it is time to move out into the world! This is where things can get tricky. This is the part that takes a lot of practice and experience. You may need to ground yourself as people often float away into the sky and have a hard time getting back down . If this happens do not panic. Simply picture heavy weights on your feet and you'll float your way back down to the ground. Always go back to your house and get back into your bed before opening your eyes.

Always return to the place where you started. Never just blink your eyes open to escape. There is nothing in this realm that can harm you so be fearless and adventurous. As you learn to navigate through the world outside of your home, down city streets, country roads and eventually up to the tops of mountains, you will begin to explore the world in a new way that has never been seen before. The world in this realm has an energetic vibration that is quite realistic. There have been people who have climbed to the tops of mountains that they never saw before to look at the flags planted. They took note of the flags and when they came back to waking life they described those flags and the funny thing is those flags actually existed on top of those mountains in the real world. It's totally possible to see things that we cannot otherwise see by doing this sort of traveling, and this is in fact traveling and the title of this meditation technique is called ASTRAL PROJECTION.

This leads us to the next segment which is also something just as hippie dippie woo woo, so be on alert!

THE AKASHIC RECORDS
THE GREAT LIBRARY OF ALL TIME AND EXISTENCE

The Akashic Records is essentially an infinite library with all the knowledge of mankind, animals, plants, the universe, all life and all existence. It has all been recorded and cataloged in this space. You get to this place through, astral projection as outlined in the previous section.

Sometimes people leave their houses during an astral projection and they are whisked away! Up through the sky, clouds, outer space and beyond everything that is noticeable. Eventually one reaches this great library. Some people see it as a great hall made of stone with giant doors leading into a lobby. This place isn't really being imagined in your own mind but it's being projected into your own projection, if that makes any sense?

So, basically you're not making this up, it's being shown to you using things from your own mind to display the awesomeness of it in a way that makes sense to you. So some people might see granite or marble floors with giant chandeliers above, some people might see it as all made of earth and plant material and some enter these great halls of light that seem to go on in all directions forever. The point is that it's a big fuckin place and it's being transmitted to you.

Okay, great. So you're there at a library, big deal right? What are you going to do about it? I drive by a real-life library almost every day but I don't go inside of it even though it has all this knowledge in it. So if you do go inside this beast of a place you'll see some strange things. It seems to be made of an infinite nature. So if you're a person seeing marble floors those floors go on for ever and ever in every direction. The rows of books go on infinitely. The shelves go up into the sky for forever. That makes it hard to find the washroom sometimes.

Inside this great hall you'll sometimes see other weird shit like these alien looking creatures, soul energies without bodies – that is, non-physical beings and other such spirits and creatures who are in there accessing the knowledge. This library contains all that ever was and all that ever will be. The story of all existence has already been written and it is there for you to discover!

You may not have the proper access to every aspect of what is contained within this library but you can surely poke around and find some very interesting things inside of there. What the fuck does that mean? Well, imagine someone from the early 1400's accessing this place and they see something simple like the first Model T Ford automobile. Their simple minds would not be able to comprehend or understand what a moving machine is or looks like and so they wouldn't understand it and they might think that magick has entered into some metals and has animated it to move about! Take that same concept for yourself and you wouldn't be able to understand the things you're seeing about the future because our minds today aren't able to comprehend the weird and wacky shit happening in the future with whatever may come.

There's no clear way to access this library after you leave your front door; not everyone is whisked away to the library and so this sort of leads us into the next section where we can talk about a certain Spaceship of sorts that has been said to carry your soul energy, your spirit, up into the higher dimensions or realms and even into the library itself!

And finally, one last segment of the ol' hippie dippie woo woo!

MERKABAH SPACESHIP MEDITATION

The Merkabah is a word used to describe a 3D representation of the Star of David, a downward pointing triangular prism merged into an upward pointing triangular prism.

To do a Merkabah Meditation, you sit with your legs crossed in a full lotus. The point of the full lotus is to have a triangular shape being made with your legs, knees and bottom. The knees make the two points of the base of this triangular prism and your ass makes the third point. From your left knee to your ass, your ass to your right knee, makes two sides of this pyramid shape and the same is happening across the front between your two knees. Your head will be at the top of the pyramid inside it and then the other triangular prism shaped structure will also be there pointing downward with the tip of its pyramid in the ground. This 'ship' is not a solid thing, it's made more of a light energy. The shape and structure carries your own energies upwards and away from your body, safely, into these other realms or dimensions without severing the connection. A severed connection supposedly causes death or leaves your body in a vegetative zombie state and this is why it's important to use a Merkabah ship for traveling beyond the astral projections.

So as we sit, we are going to focus a bright light of brilliant glowing energy coming from the top of our heads and it is shooting upwards into the heavens, into outer space, and eventually it will make a connection with one of the higher realms.

Once this connection occurs the ship will begin to float upwards carrying you inside of it until you have reached your destination. It's kinda like an elevator. Once you have reached your desired place you may be able to exit the ship. Or often times it will just go where you tell it to with your mind and you inside of it.

So now maybe you have already explored the rooms of the Library and maybe spoken with some other entities to learn something that you needed to learn and now it is time to return home.

Please keep in mind that just because you went there looking for the answers to whether or not you should marry this woman or this man, or some trivial question, does not always mean you will find the answer you were looking for. Instead, you may be presented with an answer to something else that, if you choose to accept it, will change or alter your life in some way.

Perhaps if all is written to happen that way you may end up with that wife or husband anyways. Often times you will go looking for answers and return with a greater and deeper profound knowledge and understanding. So maybe you get to see the true nature of the person you were goin to marry and you see them for who they truly are, their deeper motives. You return with that knowledge and are able to make a better informed decision about what steps to take next.

To leave, you simply walk back over to where you parked your spaceship, climb in, cross your legs and begin to think about home.

GUIDED MEDITATIONS

There are thousands of these things out there. Warning: Some are good, most are complete shit. I believe anyone could write one of these if they take the time to do it. Guided meditations aren't usually done on the fly or freestyled as that could go very wrong very quickly with just a slight hiccup if the guide didn't have a good enough imagination or a fallback plan. And so, these are usually written out beforehand and recorded, sometimes in many tries!

I always do a meditation in yoga classes that I teach with one at the each end of the class. The first one sets the stage with some hints about what the theme will be. The end meditation is straight-up like me trying to hypnotize everyone into a state of relaxation!

There are guided meditations on so many different topics out there; from eating healthier to thinking healthy thoughts about yourself to becoming better at Math and English! A lot of people listen to these at night in bed as they are falling asleep. During that time between wake and sleep we are highly suggestive and these improvement meditations kinda play around in that area.

If you would search around on Youtube you'll find a shit-tonne of these things. I would say, just start clickin on them! Eventually you'll find one that works for you. My favorite are by a fella named Jason Stephenson.

Different people value different things when it comes to these. The teacher speaking will resonate on your frequency. There are accents, the tones they use or the pace of their speaking among many other variables to what makes a good guide and these can be personal and unique to each student so I can't really tell you "Ohh, so and so is the absolute best!". For this kinda shit you gotta find it on your own. All I gotta say is to remember to not get mad at yourself when your thoughts happen because even though it's a guided thing they are still gonna get ya! We're fuckin humans man, thinking is never going to stop happening so give yourself a break and be nice to your fuckin self!

Just as an example, here is one of the guided meditations that I have written for a yoga class, there is one meditation at the beginning of class, and then another meditation at the end of the class that is split into two segments, the meditation and then "bringing them back". You will notice there are a lot of comma's to take breaks between every two or three words and this is to create a sort of hypnotic trance state with the pace as I read this from the page.

First meditation before any movement begins, for this meditation the students are sitting up with their eyes closed:

"We come into a yoga studio, and we check our lives at the door, we leave everything outside, and then we do this thing in here, and then we take this thing, and we either leave it here, or we bring it back out into the world with us, and we watch how it grows and we notice, how, subtle changes occur. If we pay attention, we can see the metaphors of yoga applied to our lives, we can see the imagery, and when we see it, we can own it, we can use it as a tool, and say yes to using it on this aspect of life but maybe not to another part. It's all up to us. As we sit here, start to feel a connection, a grounding down, while your head is light and there is an upward current of energy, pulling your body up tall, as though there was a string tied to your head, and someone is pulling on that string, lifting you up, you feel that heightening, and then all the way down below, at the base of the spine, right at the pelvic floor, there is an equal energy building, and growing, pulling you downward, this is our Root Chakra. The Root Chakra is the first Chakra on the list, located at the base of the spine, associated with the earth element, it is what connects your energetic body, with the planet. The Sanskrit name is the Muladhara Chakra, it rules over the basic needs of life, stability, food, shelter. It includes our survival instincts, a desire for safety, and security, our basic needs, of food and shelter. When these things are out of balance, you will find an imbalance in the other Chakra as well, and vice versa, when one of the lower Chakras is off, it eventually throws off the other Chakras in line above it. The other gears. To bring a balance back to your Root Chakra, we can focus on grounding, eating earthy foods, like root vegetables, keeping a small stone in your left pocket, earthing, or having your feet in the dirt, for a time, or following certain yoga poses, as outlined in today's class. Ladies and Gentlemen, without further ado, please, open your eyes, and let's get started...

This second meditation is done at the very end of class and once the students have all gotten to lay down on their backs:

As we lie on our backs, arms are floating at our sides, above the mat, gently, our palms, are facing up, we take a deep breath in, and allow it to exit softly on its own terms, breathe in together, and out, softly, in... and out.... our eyes are closed, softly, and now, relax, the arms float down to the mat, softly, feel a connection run from our hands, up our arms, from our feet, all the way up our legs, and through our backs, a connection, with the earth, beneath us, a downward connection, feel our energetic bodies, pulling us down, into the earth, a gentle tug, at our spirits, anchoring, with a weight, that not only pulls down, it is also pushing, our entire essence, deeper, and deeper, into a total, body, relaxation. Allow the mind, to wander, observe the thoughts, as they may arise, allow them to float, gently by, drifting, and then they vanish. With each, vanishing thought, we may fall ever so deeper, and deeper, back down, into a heavy, sleepy, relaxation, as the waves, of energy, wash over, we can feel, the waves, of energy, syncing, with our breath, as our chest, rises, and falls, as we breathe, and focus, on the breath, and the cleansing sound, that we make... And with each breath in, we sink, deeper, into a total, relaxation, and with each breath out, we sink, deeper, into a total, relaxation, grounding, downward, sinking... deeper, and deeper, into... ourselves...

This second segment to the final meditation is intended to bring the students back out of the meditation zone in a calm and easy way:

The energies pulling us down, begin to fade, and we feel a lightness, a weight has been lifted, *sigh*, and we begin to float, upwards, slowly, very, slowly, upwards we rise with a respected, grounding, sensation, we are always linked, with the earth beneath us. Breathing softly, we are refreshed, calm, and we feel, a sense of tranquility, and ease... We are totally, relaxed, and conscious, we are in control, of our own destinies, and we have the power, to mold, and shape, our lives. Our awareness is slowly, returning, back into the room. We first feel our feet, the air, touching them, our feet begin to twitch, and wiggle, slowly rotating, our wrists start to twitch, fingers moving, slowly, wrists can roll and wiggle, slowly, softly, and with ease, and as we count backwards to total awareness, Three, we are refreshed, Two, we are at ease, and One, we are fully alert. When you are ready, roll over onto your left side for three breaths... Now, using your right arm to prop yourself up, rise up, very, very, slowly, and we shall meet in a seated-easy pose.

Thank you, for being a part of this process, this journey, and working on your Chakras with me, may this all be reflected through your week, and weave itself into your outside lives. This week, focus on your grounding, all week long, we start at one Chakra and we work our way all the way up to the top, if we spend some time working on this, it can really straighten out our lives, or if our lives are already straightened out they can enhance what you already have. Next week we move on up to the Sacral Chakra."

And that is the end of the example of what a guided meditation would sound like from within the context of my yoga class.

POTENTIAL HINDRANCES

THE MEDITATORS ITCH

This is the first shit that happens to pretty much everyone. You're sittin there, you're doin the damn thang when suddenly out of nowhere your elbow gets itchy. And for no reason. There's no dust. There's no bugs. There ain't even like a little skin flake. But the reality is, that your elbow is itchy. So what do you do? You really wanna reach over and just give it a little scratch but that's not where we're goin. You fight through that shit. Let it sit there, be with the itch, become the fuckin itch man! Shit, don't fuckin scratch it is all I'm sayin! Cause guess what? There are two polarities at play here, two forces. You, the you who is meditating and then there's your damn body trying to snap you out of it.

Sometimes people confuse this body itch with the "ego" trying to snap you out of it. When you scratch the itch, your body goes "Ohhh! That worked! I'll do that again!" and then another itch and another until you've scratched every part of your body. With each itch scratched the meditation needs to start over.

The body is strong and it will often do these other things like muscle spasms or cramping trying to snap you out of the meditation. The body has been "Go! Go! Go!" for all of your life and now you are trying to slow it down and that muscle memory ain't liking it one bit. By practicing to ignore the itch it will go away more easily each time.

PHYSICAL PAINS

Physical pains can happen as you sit there for a long-ass time. For some people only five minutes can cause pain. Some of this pain or discomfort is still the body tryin to trick you into snappin out of the meditation.

This is where the invention of Yoga came from. Monks would sit in monasteries to meditate, to tune in with themselves and access information. They would get stiff and sore, as these monks were meditating for ten to fourteen hours each day, and so before every meditation session they would perform three or four yoga poses to stretch their backs, arms and legs in order to prepare for the long sit ahead of them.

Over time more poses were created, developed and included. This is the way of life with this sort of stuff. It starts off really simple and we complicate it. Sometimes for good reasons, sometimes not.

Simple practices were elaborated upon over time and with Yoga we now have ninety minute classes of poses with a short fifteen minute meditation at the end. Quite far removed from where it all began.

If you do some light stretches before meditation it can help to ease some of the pains that may arise. If you do yoga regularly your body will rarely have these pains anyways. If by chance during your meditation you start to feel a back ache it is perfectly okay to hang on to the knees, arch the back, sway left and right, or do circles with your torso until the pain has been calmed down and then return to the breath.

If you have muscle cramping and spasms this could be from other areas of your life such as diet and not drinking enough water. Try to stay hydrated before meditation. If cramping and spasms happen while you're meditating you may need to get up and walk around. If you need to get up it would be advised that you do a walking meditation as to not ruin your flow.

So you would get up and walk around the room with your eyes open gazing about four feet out in front of you at the floor. Eyes soft, mouth softly open, breathing slowly through your nose. Once the cramping or spasm twitches have stopped then return to your seat and return to the breath. If this happens regularly you may have some vitamin deficiencies as well and should consult your physician.

OUTSIDE SOUNDS

For a long-ass time these outside noises were the best reason for me to not meditate that day. I would wake up late and hear noises in the house from other people or noise outside and I would tell myself things like "Ahh, well, I guess today is ruined!" and I would not even try the meditation. Later on though, once I got into Binaural Beats and listening to meditation music in headphones I was able to ignore the outside world. Headphones became a crutch for me and I would use them as a reason to not meditate when I couldn't find them or if they weren't next to my bed when I woke up.

Eventually I taught myself to meditate through anything. When the city decided to start a three month construction plan right outside my window one summer I had to figure something out. The headphones and music weren't enough to drown out the jack hammers and drills and I think explosives, starting at seven AM outside my bedroom window!

So what the fuck did I do? I let the noise in. I embraced it. I welcomed that shit right into my meditation practice. I stopped using headphones and I would sit with those nasty-ass noises for the entire hour that I was then meditating for.

Yeah, at first that shit was mega annoying but eventually it all just faded away and became background noises the same as birds chirping and running water in meditation music. The noise of machinery became part of it all, a beautiful part of this world, nothing to be upset about and no reason to avoid the meditation session.

Once I had accepted that noise was going to happen no matter what I thought about it, it was easy to move on and allow it to become part of the background chatter.

Sometimes a cat would claw at my door or a roommate would make noise out in the hallway or maybe loud music was playing downstairs; through all of this I just pushed on through. POWER THROUGH IT ALL! Eventually you will begin to not even notice all of these outside annoyances as they become less of an annoyance and more of a regular part of everyday natural life on this planet. This also teaches a great lesson – that we cannot control anything in this world.

I mean, at the same time there is a level of respect that you can control by asking your family or roommates about your practice times and having a quiet time. Pets can be put away in other rooms, family can be told to keep quiet, phones can all be turned off and notices can even be placed on your doorbell if you think a parcel might arrive.

By being totally open and honest about what you are doing in there with your door shut, you can affect some positive change in this regard. However, those construction workers are getting paid to make noise from seven AM until seven PM and they are not going to stop for you so it is best to learn to live with the noise and accept it as a regular part of your meditation life.

Once you can meditate in any condition you'll never miss another session, you could potentially meditate through a fucking hurricane!

If you have conditions placed upon your practice like headphones or "no noise" you will definitely miss out on many great sessions.

CANNABIS

This is a good one. I love pot. I don't smoke that shit every day, it's just a once in a while thing for me these days after being a hardcore all-day-every-day smoker, it finally came time to take a break from that lifestyle. I am a huge proponent of cannabis as a medicine. I have achieved some amazing states meditating under the effects of cannabis and still I find that I get a much clearer and real experience without it.

With cannabis meditations I find that I get hyper-focused on one concept and the nuclear fallout of thoughts from that is incredible because I'm also quite creative and there's something about cannabis that just opens the floodgates of creativity. In a meditation session we are trying to maintain and keep the floodgates closed or at least down to a soft gentle trickle; it's hard to observe the thoughts and let them go when there are so many of them!

The only benefit is observing the flood; so many thoughts grouped together just pouring out into a river of ideas and stories and concepts. It's in that moment that you realize how silly it all is.

Having so many thoughts and thinking any one of them are more or less worthy of your constant attention is just silly. I just let them all go. And it's a beautiful thing because I used to spend my entire life fretting and worried that I had not written enough things down in one day. It was becoming a sickness. I was genuinely mad at myself for not writing things down; jokes, story ideas, blog ideas, song ideas, concepts or sometimes recording melodies I was humming into my phone.

It was nonstop. I was waking up during the night and having this chatter go through my head, like some joke ideas and I'd have to get up, turn on a bright screen, type them out and then try to get back to sleep.

Then I read this article from someone who had escaped all of this. Someone who used meditation as a way to let all of these extracurricular thoughts fade away.

They said "You don't have to do every idea that floats through your head". I had already been doing my style of meditation where I observe the thoughts and I had never considered applying this approach to my own creative actions in real life; actions I had never questioned. Like if I had a song idea I had to do it! I had to sit down and write a whole blog article and figure out a cool picture to accompany it and then with a catchy title. I just had to!

In the end, one to three people, usually nobody read them, or nobody got to hear the song. So what was all the stress about to have these things done on some sort of imaginary deadline? Over the course of nine months I slowly stopped writing everything down and eventually the idea of writing everything down seemed so foreign to me, it seemed like something a crazy person would do! Right then, I felt this pity for others who are caught in that trap followed by an elation; this weigh had been lifted!

Cannabis however, is great, and is not great. If you are someone who enjoys cannabis give it a try and then try meditating without it the next day and you will see a great difference. For some people it relaxes them or might keep the physical pains at bay but just remember that we are trying to do this on our own without any crutches to hold us up.

FOCUS TECHNIQUES

Alright, let's get back to some real learnin here! While meditation itself over time can become a good focus technique beginners may enjoy having a few more tricks up their sleeve. Here are some of the things we can do to enhance our focus and be better at tuning into the world around us while not allowing every little thing to become a distraction.

CREAT A TECH-FREE ZONE

Our gadgets are here to save us time and often we end up wasting more time because of them. Our cell phones have become an extension of our bodies and this can affect our attention spans and our relationships with others. Establishing a room in your home that will not be allowed to have any technology in it will greatly affect the way you are able to focus on the present moment. Since that room is a tech-free zone nobody will ever go into that room and it will become a great quiet space for your meditation practice.

GET YOUR ASSES OUTSIDE!

Even if you live in a busy city ten minutes in a park every two days will work wonders to reset your system. Leave everything at home like the dog, your cellphone (Maybe on airplane mode if you are doing this park-time on your lunch breaks). Have at least ten minutes in nature free from distractions other than birds and squirrels and the sound of the leaves in the trees.

MAKE A LIST OF WHAT STIMULATES YOU

What are your core distractions?

You don't gotta try and stop the distractions cause that shit is nearly impossible but by becoming aware of the things that stimulate you will alter the way they affect you.

For me one of the greatest things I have ever done was taking marketing courses in college. This opened up my eyes to the subliminal trickery happening on a day to day basis with advertisers and their marketing. The lights in stores, the colors used on packaging and even the characters or fonts on packaging is all playing a major part trying to catch your attention and to distract you from your original intent. We've all done it before in the past when we went to the store for bread and came out with everything but bread. Recognizing and realizing these distractions exist allows us to break free from the pattern of control they hold over us as we become more mindful of their presence. Distractions are distractions no matter what they are or how you look at them and they are the same for your shopping experience or for your meditation sessions.

KEEP TWO SEPARATE DO-DO LISTS

Write one long list that helps you clear your head of the many thoughts that may pop into your mind such as "Pick up the dry cleaning, dog food and go to the teacher conference on your way home from yoga class today". This to-do list can be as long as you like but keep it out of sight.

The second to-do list should only contain the top priority three items from your long list and as each item gets checked off you can add one more from the long list.

PAY ATTENTION TO YOUR GEAR-SWITCHING
(Previously known as Multitasking)

Multitasking can help boost your brain when you are working on a boring task however it has a negative side effect because of our brain's plasticity or the way our brains change in response to experiences we have. When your brain changes itself to favor divided attention and fragmented thoughts, we become more prone to distractions on a regular basis. By not engaging in too much gear-switching our brains are better able to focus on the task that is directly in front of us, one thing at a time, and it will more quickly rebound from distractions.

A few little games you can play at home include:

STARING AT A CIRCLE

Take a black marker and draw a circle on a sheet of paper about three or four inches wide. If you have poor circle drawing skills you can always print one out from your computer from Google Images. The paper is attached to the wall in front of you far enough away that you can sit on the either the floor or a chair and stare at it without the circle being out of focus or blurred. You should generally be about three to four feet away from it for most people.

The task of this exercise is to stare at the circle without allowing your eyes to lose focus – without allowing the circle to start to double, shake, blur or move around any. Whenever it starts to do this simply blink and adjust. Do this for anywhere between five and ten minutes every few days. Once you have the visual aspect down perhaps try and include thoughts by thinking of only the circle and when your thoughts begin to wander and you start going over your long to-do list bring them back to the circle. Even just saying the word "Circle" repeatedly would work.

VISUALIZATION PRACTICES

These are things such as astral projection. We have already outlined this technique and it is a great method to help focus your mind on one thing at a time as you complete your entire body scans. There are also thousands of guided meditations online that you can listen to for free, on Youtube for example, that will guide your mind and your focus through a selected time-frame. Choose one that suits you the most and run with it, or I guess technically 'sit' with it! You can even write your own guided focus meditations if you are so creatively inclined. Simple things like counting from one to ten and then reversed from ten to one can also help build your brain up into a one-thing-at-a-time routine for focusing on the task in front of you.

HOLD AN IMAGE IN YOUR MIND

Sit, stand or lie down with your eyes closed and try to hold an unwavering image in your mind. To start try using the black circle from your sheet. Eyes are closed, see the circle, see its color, its diameter, its circumference. Try to hold its shape in your mind for as long as possible and eventually you can work up to more complex geometric shapes or even symbols. Later on, leading you to hold images of people or things or places. When your mind starts to wander just go back to the circle.

FOCUS

If you have ever used a magnifying glass to burn anything you know how focus works. The light is wide and blurred at first and as you adjust the angle and position of the glass the light becomes more clearly defined and solid with a brighter glow and sharp edges. As you sit, stand or lie down with your eyes closed picture this entire process happening from start to end. Once you are able to control the focus of this light from within, your mind will start to add some things that you can maybe burn, like a piece of wood, where once the focus is held for the count of ten you can picture the wood starting to darken and smoke. Eventually you can get creative and write your name in the wood; I like to write a nice cuss word, those always make me feel better, nothing says you love yourself like the "Fuck" word burned into a soft cedar plank!

There are many more focus techniques available online if you dig around, these ones should be enough for you to get started. I started with the circle on a wall technique way back when I was only sixteen years old.

MAGICK!

(Wait... What? Really?)

And now for one of my favorite segments: The hippiest dippiest woo wooiest bullshit of all!

It is believed that through yoga and meditation, over time, we can awaken these latent sleeping psychic abilities. Now, this is kinda "out there" and I understand if nobody wants to believe any of this shit so you can just go ahead and close the fucking book, that's why this shit is here at the very end!

So let's use our famous example again: There you are driving to work, again, and some JERK-HOLE just cut you off "Aarrghhh!". And you wish you could just put your hands to your temples and "Na-na-na-na-na-na" Plop! Flatten that motherfuckers tires!

So you go home and you start digging around online and you find out that through yoga and meditation you can potentially develop these abilities. Now, here's the catch, in order to achieve these powers the process to get there will completely change who you are, how you think and how you look at the world to the point where you are no longer an angry person who wants to flatten someones tires.

You'll be able to see the galactic whole; you'll understand maybe that guy was racing his wife to the hospital as she is having a baby in the back seat, so of course, being cut off is not going to anger you and you are not going to magickally flatten the guys tires on him and instead you simply pull aside and let him pass. So the people who have achieved these powers do not need to use them and do not want to use them because they have become these pure angelic creatures.

Sometimes, as is the case with many Gurus who are these enlightened beings, these miracles start to happen all around them but never on command. You don't see a Guru moving a mountain to show off to his girlfriend. These things only happen when it is important for the flow of this story of earth to continue in such a way that it will help other people on their journey.

One of the best examples is a psychologist from Harvard back in the 1960's named Dr. Richard Alpert who went to India. Dr. Alpert went up on a hilltop and he lay there at night looking up at the stars and he was thinking about his mother back in New York.

The next day they took him to meet the Guru. Alpert had no desire to meet a Guru. He had no interest in Hindu mumbo jumbo. "Those charlatans with their snake oils" he thought. Still, not to be rude, he met the Guru Maharaji, and Maharaji said to him "Ahh, so you laid up on the mountain last night?" and the Doctor said "Yes I did (Hmm, yeah anyone could have seen me up there and told this guy that!)" and the Guru said "Ahh, and you were looking up at the stars?" and the Doctor said "Yes Maharaji, I was looking at the stars (Like what else does one do laying on the hill at night?)". And then the Guru said "And you were thinking about your mother back in New York" and the Doctor just stopped in his tracks.

Maharaji continued to tell the Doctor private and personal things that he had never told anyone before out loud. Things from inside his own mind. This "miracle" event spawned one of the greatest proponents of Hinduism. One of the largest names to ever emerge from India, for that night he may have climbed up the mountain as a fancy Harvard professor with credentials and a title and initials before his name, but he came down that mountain as a changed being and was furthermore known as Baba Ram Dass.

Today Ram Dass has written countless books, performed thousands of hours of seminars all across North America and really brought all of this Eastern mysticism here to the West. And it's not like the Guru was sitting there going "Hey watch me screw with this Westerner with my powers!". No, he did not do it on purpose, it would just happen and it would happen when the time was right.

I highly recommend any Ram Dass books if you wish to continue with any of this stuff starting with "Be Love Now" and then go back and read its prequel "Be Here Now". Reading them in reverse order makes a lot more sense if you ask me.

And so, there are many other stories of Gurus and other spiritual people and non-spiritual people who have claimed to have these powers. It's never the people themselves who make this claim it is always the people around them who hoist them up on this platform. As I mentioned before once someone has reached this area of "being" they do not want to interfere on purpose and have every scientist on earth dissecting them in a lab.

YOUR MISSION

(Should you choose to accept it!)

One minute per day, at the same time each day.

If you someday feel like you want a little more then by all means do a little more, but at least do one minute.

Make this the first thing you do each day so if you need to wake up one minute earlier then set your alarm one minute earlier. Sit up in your bed and do the one minute of meditation.

Set an alarm for the one minute and make sure it's nothing to disruptive, I recommend a nice bell, chimes or a solid tone.

That is everything!

Y'all are well on your way to becoming meditation experts!

If you have any questions regarding this book or any of the little struggles you are having or maybe you just want to say hello, send an email to jay@jaycoleyoga.ca and I will do my best to help you in any way that I can!

So for now, so long folks,
Peace, Love and Light,
Namaste, and all that other good noise!
DING!

ABOUT THE AUTHOR

Jason started meditating at the early age of nine to escape the sibling rivalries with his brother and sister during summer vacations. Jason holds a Doctorate in Metaphysics from the ULC, Modesto California. He is an artist working in fine art with pencil drawings, paintings and craft works. Jason lived as a graphic designer running his own small marketing company from an early age up into his twenties. Afterward Jason became one of the pioneering hiphop artists in his home province of New Brunswick, Canada. Eventually Jason started doing Stand-Up Comedy for a short five year run. After living all of his dreams Jason became a certified Yoga Instructor in Canada where he has been teaching, doing a podcast called Beyond the Mat, and running his small cleaning company, YogiClean. A quote from a book called The Peaceful Warrior played in the movie adaptation by Nick Nolte that has always resonated with Jason, is:

"There is no greater purpose, than the service of others."

Please stay tuned for more great works by Dr. Jason Cole as there are two unpublished fantasy fiction novels waiting to see the light of day!

www.ingramcontent.com/pod-product-compliance
Lightning Source LLC
Chambersburg PA
CBHW021207020426
42331CB00003B/241